The Cracked Pot

A play

Blake Morrison

Translated and adapted from
Heinrich von Kleist's *Der Zerbrochene Krug*

Samuel French — London
New York - Toronto - Hollywood

The Broken Jug

First performed at the West Yorkshire Playhouse, Leeds, on 23rd February, 1995, with the following cast of characters:

Bright	Paul McCrink
Judge Adam	Barrie Rutter
Aunt Bridget/Maid	June Broughton
Judge Walter	John Branwell
Eve Rudd	Cathy Sara
Martha Rudd	Kate Rutter
Leslie Dixon	Andrew Cryer
Tommy Dixon	Andrew Livingston

Directed by **Barrie Rutter**
Designed by **Polly Richards**
Lighting by **Chris Brockhouse**

CHARACTERS

Adam, town judge
Walter, visiting magistrate from the High Court in Manchester
Bright, clerk to the court
Martha, plaintiff
Eve, Martha's daughter
Tommy Dixon, a farmer
Leslie, Tommy Dixon's son
Aunt Bridget, witness
Meg, a maid

Place: the town courtroom, also Judge Adam's house, in Skipton, in the West Riding of Yorkshire

Time: circa 1810

Preface

The German master at Ermysted's Grammar School, Skipton, Yorkshire, in the late 1960s, was a tall, kindly, rather weary Englishman called Dick Dulling. Perhaps his weariness came from his having to teach our recalcitrant little A-level group of four. With our adolescent awkwardness and Craven vowels, we were not great linguists, and the pronunciation of long German sentences - which Peter de Vries once compared to the sound of suitcases falling downstairs - did not come easily to us. I was the least natural linguist of all, and in two years my only real pleasure came from studying a novel by Heinrich Böll and a play by Heinrich von Kleist. Sadly the literature element of the course was tiny, and I finished up with a mediocre A-level and the belief that all German writers were called Heinrich.

I never forgot about Kleist's *Der Zerbrochene Krug*, though. I remembered that Kleist had got the idea for it from an old copper engraving he'd seen in Switzerland showing a judge, a frightened girl, an old woman with a jug, and a young man accused of breaking it. I remembered that the play has sometimes been called the only comedy in the German language. I remembered the great central role, the village judge, Adam, who's both hearty and brainy, corrupt and manipulative, Falstaffian and Machiavellian. I even remembered that part of the plot has to do with a club foot - *Klumpfuss*. In the 1970s, hitch-hiking in Greece, I was picked up by a German doctor who actually had a club foot and I spent the day trying not to show off the one arcane German word in my limited vocabulary.

Kleist had a way of dropping into my life - though he dropped out of his own tragically early, in a suicide pact with a terminally ill woman, at 34. So when I was asked to translate *Der Zerbrochene Krug* by the Royal National Theatre (the plain National Theatre as it was then) in the late 1980s, I jumped at the chance. The National had asked Tony Harrison first, but he had told them : "No, I'm an urban Yorkshire poet; you need rural Yorkshire - try Blake Morrison". Richard Eyre was keen to revive the play, and to direct it himself, as he'd done at least once before. His hope was to give Kleist's blank verse a strongly vernacular quality, a northern accent. I approved of that: I wanted to bring it back home to Skipton.

Unfortunately, owing to heavy schedules, the play wasn't done at the National. But in 1993 Barrie Rutter, of Northern Broadsides, commissioned me to have another go - and to make greater use of the kind of dialect I'd used in the narrative poem *The Ballad of the Yorkshire Ripper*. There is a rich seam of wonderfully expressive old Yorkshire words, and mining it is not to dabble in nostalgia but to tap still-living energies. Many of the 4,000 dialect words collected in 1911 by Richard Blakeborough for his book *Yorkshire Wit, Character, Folklore and Customs* were still in use when I was growing up, and it was natural to turn to these when bringing Kleist to the West Riding. Several versions later here the play finally is, no longer a broken jug but a cracked pot.

In Kleist's lifetime *Der Zerbrochene Krug* had only one production, directed by Goethe - a disaster, by all accounts (including Kleist's), in part because it was done slowly and stiltedly, with two intervals. But Kleist remained fond of the play, and said : "To a very astute friend, it may well pass for an imprint of my being". Though he set it in Utrecht in 1770, he wrote it in the first decade of the nineteenth century, and this is where *The Cracked Pot* now takes place, in a small town something like Skipton, and at a time when old ways were going and railways (and canals, mills, factories) were coming in.

The tension between Judge Adam and the visiting magistrate from Manchester, Walter, is in part a clash between old and new. But there's also a more local rivalry, between Yorkshire and Lancashire, white rose and red rose, the history of which is depicted on the eponymous cracked pot. That regional rivalry continues to this day. Perhaps it is as timeless as all the other human character-istics which Kleist explored in his play, and which I hope I've also explored in this reworking.

Blake Morrison

I like knowing poets: after all they are professional word-writers and I'm a professional word-speaker, so when their craft moves into the Theatre the friendship and partnership receives public acclaim. This was exactly the case with *The Cracked Pot*. I read Blake's first draft of the then called *Broken Jug* on the recommendation of Tony Harrison. A change of title and eleventen drafts later *The Cracked Pot* met its own local audience in a Yorkshire playhouse.

It's a matter of public record that the play became an instant classic. Blake now receives at least one idea a month from me - as well as his own constructive trawling - hoping to stir his juices in a further celebration of the glories of language that he brought to *Cracked Pot*! The anticipation is sweet. Yes, I like knowing poets.

Barrie Rutter
Artistic Director
Northern Broadsides

SELECTED GLOSSARY

batter-fanged beaten by a woman
belder roar like a bull
bellytimber food
bensiling chastisement
bizzumhead foolish person
blair shout
blathry muddy
blish-blash gossip
bowdykite cheeky child
brock badger
brully squabble
buzznacking gossip
caff-hearted cowardly
caggy dirty, quarrelsome
caufhead stupid fellow
chaffer, chunter bicker, complain
clarty sticky, clumsy
clunter heavy fall
crammly twisted
creepins shivering fear
daddly intoxicated
differing bout quarrel
dirty-bottomed untrustworthy
dodderums violent shakings
drabbletail loose woman
dunderknowle stupid person
flappytongue gossip
flaumy tawdry
fustilugs low fellow
gammerstang whore
garfits entrails
gee-gaws jewels
gowky clumsy
grenky ugly

griming cover
hauvey-gauvey lout
honey-fall rare piece of luck
lig lie
murl melt
nauping thrashing
nazz-moll immoral woman
nazzled drunk
nobbut middling unwell
owerance command
prickyback hedgehog
rafflepack riotous assembly
ragabash, ragally rough fellow
rantipole romping child
ruddock robin
scutters diarrhoea
splaudy wide-spreading
splunder burst
swintways diagonal
timber-toed wearing a wooden leg
tongue-scraping flattery
trail-tripe whore
traps belongings
Tyke Yorkshireman
whiffle-waffle idle talk

ACT I

SCENE 1

Adam is sitting/lying on the edge of his bed, head in hands

Bright enters

Bright Bedfast, sir? You're not sickening for summat?
Adam I've come a right clunter this time, brainbox.
Bright You fell, you mean, sir?
Adam   Fell, aye, fell down a fell
  To judge from t'pain I'm in.
Bright   It puts me in mind
  Of a namesake of yours, your ancestor,
  Who had *his* fall before t'world began.
  A little food, a woman, temptation,
  Then woomph, a snakepit, disaster. Ring any bells?
Adam You're talking balls, boy. *That's* where I fell,
  On t'floor.
Bright   So it weren't last night?
Adam   No, just now.
Bright And you weren't speaking figuratively?
Adam Look, when I say spade I don't mean shovel.
  It were summat like a spade sent me flying.
  Now my head feels like a grave that's freshly dug.
Bright So how did it happen, sir?
Adam   How do you think?
  How do folks normally fall out of bed?
  There I am, getting up, full of t'jummocks
  Of spring, singing at t'top of my voice,
  When I trip and fall flat on my face.
  I'm told I sing flat—maybe it serves me right.
Bright Ah, t'right. (*He points to Adam's foot*)

Adam   Right?
Bright   No, I bet it were left.
Adam Left? Leave it out.
Bright   You know, your … okkerd foot.
Adam What in t'midden are you on about?
Bright   The … club foot.
Adam Club foot? My two feet club along together
Fine, thanks. Where t'one leads, t'other follows,
Unless I've had a potful and they part company.
Bright It looks like you were nazzled last night. (*He brings him a mirror*)
Adam   Crudding tuptails!
I'm like a sheep that's just been fleeced—my skin's
Riddled with cuts where t'farmer's shears have dug in.
Bright I'd say you were on t'bevy in t'Black Horse
And got into a scrap with t'whole of taproom.
Adam If you think I'm bad, you should have seen t'rest.
No, t'scrap I had was with that bloody goat
On t'corner of t'range. That's right, you know how it is.
I trip, and pitch forrad, then clutch at t'air
Just like a bloke does when he's daddly.
As I slip I make a grab for t'britches
Which I've hung on t'clothes-horse here to dry.
Two legs are dangling down like stirrups, see,
And I've got hold, I'm safe I think, then rip,
They tear, t'saddle slips, t'clothes-horse panics and rears,
Then bolts across floor dragging me wi' it,
I'm clinging on for life under its belly,
Till wap, it hoofs me one here on t'nut,
And sends me galloping backwards, I'm flying
Through t'air again, no stopping me now I think,
Jerusalem here I come, when, woomph, boomph,
I stop dead, I fetch up here on t'range
Just where yon goat's sticking out his horns.
Not little nubs neither, more like antlers
They felt when they splundered into my skull.
Trampled underfoot by a clothes-horse
Then butted in t'head by a cast-iron goat:
That's me, mauled near to death by dead animals.
Bright Bravo. Great comic performance, sir.

Adam Comic? Wi' all this pain? More like tragedy.
Bright High farce, then. Not t'first time Adam's fallen
Either, but t'first time *outside* of bed.
Adam By God, aye, brainbox. Anyway, what's up?
Bright What's up? Oh aye, sorry, I almost forgot.
Get ready for the visiting magistrate.
Adam The what?
Bright   Judge Clegg's coming, from Manchester.
He's on an inspection tour of t'Riding.
And today he's visiting us.
Adam   Us? Today?
You're having me on, thruster. What's t'date,
April First, is it?
Bright   True as I stand here,
Honest. He were just up t'road in Ilkley,
Yesterday. And I saw Dick Manby first thing,
Hitching up his cart to go and fetch him here.
Adam Hold on to your horses, lad. Fetch him here?
Who's he think he is, hoity-toitying it?
If he'd wrote to say he were visiting
I'd have told him to come by Embsay Moor
And wi' luck t'bugger would never have got here.
Bright He did write. I left this letter on your desk
A fortnight ago—have you not read it?
Adam Bah, we've had these before.
Bright   Look at t'signature,
Though. It's not your old mate Judge Pickles
From Ripon. That's done wi', the old pals' act,
It's been repealed, it went out wi' t'last century.
It's Judge Walter Clegg now, from Manchester,
And Manchester's answerable to London.
Adam Keep your hair on. It's Judge bleeding Walter Clegg:
So what? He weren't born yesterday, were he?
He's sworn his oath of office, hasn't he?
He must know how we run t'law round here.
All right, he's from Manchester, but he's human.
I'll bet he knows when to look t'other way
And that he'll not say "no" to a noggin or two.
Bright Well, I can tell you he went through Ilkley

Like a handful of lime—sat in on a trial,
Examined t'books, suspended Judge Crocker,
And appointed his clerk to take over.
Well, so Dick Manby were told, any road.
Adam Dick Manby told you all this, did he?
Bright Aye, and more. Judge Crocker tried to top himself.
Adam Tried? He's still living?
Bright   Aye, but his career's dead.
Adam Crocker weren't dishonest, you know, only sloppy.
That must have been his downfall: carelessness.
So, brainbox. Let's just stick together, eh.
You know how t'world works: you stand by me,
You give me a leg-up when I need one,
And one day I'll do t'same for you. You know
How I've always encouraged you, thruster:
Paid for you to take that correspondence course,
Sent you to those elocution lessons
In Huddersfield, passed on my bookkeeping skills.
I don't ask for gratitude, only patience.
You'd like to be a judge yourself, I know that.
But t'wise man knows when to keep his trap shut.
Thickness goes for nowt if t'rope's too short.
Bright Me, sir, the ambitious sort? You don't think…?
Adam I'll retire one day, then you can take over.
But for now, remember, I'm t'judge here.
Oh, I've my faults, I'll not pretend different.
But why should a judge, when he's not sitting,
Be as white and upright as a polar bear?
Bright I take your point, sir. I'm with you there.
Adam Well, then, old son. Let's get these papers sorted,
Before *he* arrives, this Walter Clegg chap:
My legal files are piled as high as Shap.

Meg enters

Morning, Margaret—what can we do for you?
Meg Morning, sir. There's a lad at t'front door,
Says he's a message from Judge Walter Clegg,
Confirming his appointment this morning.

He's been held up but hopes to be here sharp.
Adam Ruddocks and brocks, you mean he's nearly here?
Meg That's the nub, sir.
Adam   My clothes then, Meg, and quick.
Bright Tell the lad m'lud's most welcome here
  And we're deeply honoured to receive him.
Adam Like hell we are. If you tell him anything
  Tell him I've asked to be excused.
Bright   Excused?
Adam Aye, excused. How long did the lad say he'd be?
Meg He's stuck at t'Devonshire Arms, sir,
  Waiting for t'blacksmith. His coach had a bump.
  The axle were damaged and needs fixing.
Adam Good, excellent. The smith's a lazy sod.
  Wi' luck it'll take him hours to fettle it.
  Now, Meg, let's have some decent grub laid on—
  Wensleydale, ham, meat pies, a jug of beer.
Bright Had a bump, the lad said? Was Judge Clegg injured?
Meg Nowt to speak of: cricked his neck a bit, that's all.
Adam Pity he didn't break it.
Bright   Cricked his neck!
  Tell the lad to send Judge Clegg our condolences.
Adam Just get t'food first, Meg: don't rush the lad.
  He can send our message back soon enough.
  (*To Bright*) What's up with you, old son? Don't fret so much.
Bright How do you mean?
Adam   I mean, don't get so flustered.
Bright What, me?
Adam   Now then, Meg, what's that you've brought us?
Meg Sausages, sir.
Adam   Wrong, them's the wardship files.
Bright   Me, flustered?
Adam Take them back to my desk.
Meg   The sausages?
Adam No, you dummy, the papers they were wrapped in.
Bright Me, flustered?
Meg   All right, but I can't find your wigs.
  I've searched your desk but neither of em's there.
Adam Why not?

Meg   One's gone missing since yesterday, sir.
And t'other must still be back at t'wigmakers.
Adam Right. I want you to go round to Parson Blacklaw
And ask if he'll borrow me his. Say the cat
Used mine to drop its kittens in last night
And I've not seen it since.
Bright   Are you spinning us one?
Adam Have you ever kenned me to lie? Five kittens.
Bright In the wig?
Adam   I'd hung it over t'chair last thing, see.
Bright The cat then took it in her mouth…
Adam   Happen, aye.
Bright …Dragged it behind your bed and had kittens.
Adam In t'wig, aye. They're buggers are cats, you know,
Have it off here, have it off there, drop young uns
Anywhere.
Bright   But t'kittens must be around somewhere.
Adam They were just a tick since. Kitty-kitty!
Five. Two black, two orange, and a white one.
Bright And t'wig?
Adam   Must have gone walkies wi' 'em.
Meg So shall I be off to Parson Blacklaw, sir?
Adam Aye, and my greetings to Mrs Blacklaw, too.
Tell her I'll be round to visit very soon.

Meg exits

I don't like it, Bright, I don't like it.
Bright   What, sir?
Adam I feel everything's pitched against me.
I've slept badly. My head hurts. I've no wig.
Ooh, and t'dreams I've had—I feel tom-flogged by 'em,
They were that grenky I'm scared to shut my eyes.
And why would it have to be our weekly session
When this Walter Clegg-Legg comes snouting around?
Bright But that's the point, sir—to see you in command,
To prove how you've owerance ower t'law.
Adam A waste of his time. I don't need to be
Weighed up like this. Let me be my own judge.

Bright By t'sound of it there's a good crowd any road,
So you can put on a bit of a show...

SCENE 2

Walter enters

Walter Good day to you, Judge Adam.
Adam   Greetings, m'lud.
Felicitations from little Skipton.
We had no idea, we'd never have presumed
To hope for the pleasure of such a visit,
It's beyond our wildest imaginings—
Before even ten in the morning, what's more.
Walter I realize it's all a bit new to you,
This government inspection procedure.
But let me set your mind at rest. I've found,
Going about my work in the Ridings,
That there's as much pleasure to it as business.
And my hosts, when I leave them, mean it
Quite sincerely when they wish me on my way.
Adam I'm sure they do. I'm sure we'll do t' same.
Walter I must emphasise there's nothing sinister
In my visit. I hear good things of Skipton.
Adam We do our best, m'lud, our humble best.
Work and more work, that's how we do things here.
Fortune's best getten with a wet shirt.
Walter The High Court in Manchester is concerned
That standards of justice be sternly upheld
Throughout the Ridings. Certain abuses
Are known to us already, and offenders
Will be dealt with severely.
Adam   Like my colleague
In Ilkley, m'lud: I heard you dealt with him.
Walter That was a case of gross embezzlement.
My visit *here* should be a formality.
My brief is to observe, not to punish.
If some things are not exactly to the letter,

You'll not find me a pedant: I'm happy
If the spirit's being observed.
Adam   Spirit, aye:
Glad to hear it. I too believe in spirit.
A most commendable philosophy, m'lud.
You'll find no doubt we occasionally fall short
In small ways here and there, through adhering
Too closely to the ancient ways of the town.
Oh, I know people fret to make changes.
Revolution's all the rage and everyone's
A clever clogs who knows his Diderot,
His Rousseau and Montesquieu and Voltaire.
Well, *chacun à son gout*, that's what I say,
Each to his own gout: Skipton isn't France.
We try to stay abreast—we've had our first mill
Open not long since—but there's a limit.
It takes me all my time just keeping up.
For every one law that was, there are three now.
That's progress for you.
Walter   I do take your point.
These new laws could really do with some sifting.
Adam Sifting? You'd need a whacking great sieve.
It's chaff, this new-fangled stuff, pure chaff.
Walter Well, not chaff entirely, there's some sustenance.
And this, I presume, must be your clerk.
Bright Wilfred Bright, your must humble servant, m'lud.
Is your neck all right? We heard you'd been hurt.
Walter My neck—that was nothing.
Bright   I could bind it up,
Or we could fetch t'doctor for you.
Adam   Doc Laycock?
Are you half-rocked? T'last person he called on's
Laid out in t'ground wi' a lily in each hand.
Walter Have you been with Judge Adam long, Mr Bright?
Bright It'll be fourteen year this June, m'lud.
Walter Fourteen years as clerk? I'd have thought by now…
Adam Take a pew, your lordship, you must be tired.
Walter It's all right.
Adam   I insist: you've crossed the Pennines.

It takes it out of a man, climbing hills.

Walter But only from Ilkley this morning...

Adam Did you not look at the Cow and Calf, then?

Walter Cow and Calf?

Adam   Two boulders, sir, on Ilkley Moor,
Sort of nuzzling up, famous in these parts.

Walter Yes, yes. We must have a word about your clerk,
You know, after court, when we look at your books.
First, though, how many taxes do you collect?

Adam Let me think, eight, isn't it, Bright?

Walter   *Eight?*

Adam Yes. One, there's the land registration tax.
Two, the candle tax. Three, the newspaper tax.
Four, windows—daylight robbery, they call it.
Five, the hay, silage and muck-spreading tax.

Walter That's a new one on me.

Adam   And on the farmers,
Your lordship, but where there's shit there's shillings. Six,
The Leeds-Liverpool Canal flood relief tax.

Walter The Leeds-Liverpool Canal flood relief tax?
I didn't know they'd built the canal yet.

Adam Happen they've not, sir, your side of the border.
Skipton to Bingley's been open thirty year.
It were t'first stretch: we were pioneers.
If only Lancashire would pull its weight
Like our Yorkshire horses pull their barges.

Walter But a flood? Surely...

Adam   It's been known, your lordship.
Seven is the Clitheroe-Keighley turnpike toll tax.

Walter It seems a lot...

Adam   ...of paperwork, aye.

Walter   And eight?

Adam Eight is t'tithes which farmers pay to t'squire,
But which since his infirmity I take instead
And put to use at my own discretion.

Walter Um, most irregular. But if the squire
Himself is happy...

Adam   Oh, he's happy enough.
Since he went mental, he's delirious.

Walter I'll look into this more closely later.
  But now to business. First you must show me…
Adam Show you t'town, m'lud? With pleasure. Now t'castle's
  Long been in t'hands of t'Clifford family…
Walter No, you misunderstand. I meant, show me
  How the law is administered here,
  In a court session.
Bright   That's right, it's after ten.
Walter And that crowd of people waiting outside,
  I take it that they…
Adam   Oh, them…
Bright   Yes, indeed, m'lud,
  · They're the plaintiffs waiting.
Adam   Well done, brainbox.
Walter Good, good, that suits my purpose, gentlemen.
  Let them in, in the usual way. As for me,
  I'll take a back seat and let you get on.
Adam A back seat? Never—you must be elevated,
  You must sit at my right hand and observe
  That everything's done right, (*aside*) God slit your throat.
Walter That's very kind—I'll just sit and take the odd note.

  Meg enters

Meg Parson Blacklaw's wife sends her best, sir.
  She'd have liked to come up trumps wi' a wig,
  But her husband's gone to Bradford wi' it
  To preach a sermon…
Adam   The big, daft, jumped-up,
  Never-come-down, pious, Protestant,
  Pulpit-pumping, ploaky-faced potwaller.
Meg She says if you can hang on she'll send it later.
Adam No good, I can't. I may as well come clean, m'lud…
Walter What's this?
Adam   One of those things, a spot of bad luck,
  Has meant I'm without both my wigs. Now a third's
  Gone, too, that I was due to lay my hands on.
  I'm going to have to sit bare-headed in court.
Walter Bare-headed?

Adam   Bare as Adam came into t'world,
Which may mean sacrificing a little
Of my usual dignity, but then again
Good behaviour never needs a drainpipe.
Walter But without a wig... What about the parson?
Adam No, he's off preaching with his in Bradford.
Walter Or the schoolteacher?
Adam   The schoolteacher?
Ah no, m'lud. I used to rent him out my wig,
And my gown, but he took umbrage, you see,
Said I were charging too much—they're not well off,
Teachers, short of brass and getting shorter:
No, there'll be no help from that quarter.
Walter So what do you propose? The court is waiting.
Do you plan to procrastinate till your hair grows back?
Adam If you'll allow me, I'll send Meg to a farm.
I've an idea young Harry Watson has a wig.
Walter How long will that take?
Adam   Only a couple of hours.
Walter A couple of hours! But we're already late.
In that case, you must proceed...
Adam   Proceed. Really?
Walter You'll just have to put some powder on your head
And make the best of it. I can't waste more time.
Adam Nor me, worse luck. Right then, onwards and upwards—
Though I confess I'm nobbut middling today.
Walter Dear, dear. I hope nothing too serious.
Do you feel fit enough to go ahead?
I could always ask your clerk to step in.
Adam M'lud, a lesser man might take to his bed.
I'm hoarse as a raven and parched as a sponge,
But I'll not be diverted from the road
To justice.
Walter   Most commendable, Judge Adam.
Adam But first let me show you t' privy, m'lud:
Calls of nature mustn't be ignored.

Adam and Walter exit

SCENE 3

Martha, Eve, Tommy and Leslie enter

Tommy Oh, stop chuntering, woman. Offer's on t'table.
  Like I say, if my Leslie smashed thy pot
  Tha'll get thi compensation. We'll sort it out.
Martha Sort it out? My jug? Get on wi' thee.
  How can tha sort my jug out now it's gone to pot
  For good? It's that son of yours needs sorting out,
  Him with his clarting great hands who broke it.
Tommy Don't get thi rag out, Martha. We've argified
  And argy-barged enough. If it turns out
  What tha's saying sticks, I'll see thee right, all right?
Martha If what I'm saying sticks, you'll seem me right?
  And how'll you do that when you're at home?
  Stick it back on t'mantelpiece, is that right?
  Or stick t'pieces back together, is that right?
  Dost tha think Judge Adam's a potter,
  Who can stick all t'broken bits on his wheel
  And whirl 'em round till they're in one piece again?
  You know where you can stick them ideas.
  Your Leslie hasn't got a leg to stand on,
  No more than my jug has. It in't even fit
  To be a pisspot now.
Leslie   Nay, it's thee's full of piss.
Tommy Come on, we're not here for a differing bout.
  Advising them that's in a passion
  Is dafter than scratching a tup's head.
  We've chaffered enough: now it's time for t'judge.
Leslie It in't t'crack in t'pot that's narking her, Dad,
  It's t'hole in t'middle of her wedding plans.
  She's trying to scare me into patching it up.
  Well, she's riding a dead nag. Me marry Eve?
  That two-timing sludge? I'd sooner wed a coot.
Martha You great bizzum-head. I don't give a hoot
  About your wedding. It in't worth one shard
  Of my jug and I'll not waste my breath trying
  To fix it. If Eve's wedding were that jug of mine,

There's nowt I'd enjoy more than hurling it
Straight in tha gob, you great gowky dunderknowle.
Patch up thy wedding? Good shuttance, I say.

Tommy Aye, me and all. There's more folks wed than keep
Good houses, and these two are still hanging
In t'bell-ropes. I'll get t'brass back on t'ring yet.

Eve Leslie.

Leslie   Sod off.

Eve   Leslie, love.

Leslie   I said, sod off.

Eve Please, Leslie.

Leslie   Tha were saying please last night
But it weren't to me, tha little trail-tripe.

Eve Please, there's something I've got to say, in secret.

Leslie There in't no secrets wi' you any more:
All t' lot's wide open.

Eve   I'm not listening to you.
It's you who should be listening to me.
You know you might get the call-up soon, to war,
And who knows, once you're humping a gun about
Whether we'll ever see each other again.
War, war against Bonaparte, think what it means.
Do you want to go off bearing grudges?

Leslie Grudges? Nay, I'll not bear thee grudges, Eve,
Or stand in thy way. Any man can have thee now,
Happen most round here have had thee already.
Tha took me for a ride, while tha gave them one.
So don't talk to me about war. Do you think
I care if I die any more, you little buer?
They can stick me through wi' a bayonet.
It'll be nowt to what's been stuck up you.

Martha Come away from him. What did I tell thee?
Have you ever heard such filth in all your life?
His brass is all in his face, not his pocket.
I'll find thee a nice young corporal, pet,
Not that ragally wi' his mucky mouth,
That buzznacking, caff-hearted bletherhead...

Eve Mam, Mam, don't take on, it's not worth it.
I'll get your pot fixed by somebody in town.

And if that's no good I'll use up my savings
To buy you a new one. Could any pot,
Even if it went back to Herod, be worth this fuss?
Let's go home: we're courting disaster here.
Martha Nay, your courting him were t'disaster
And we've come to court to put things right.

Walter enters

My jug wouldn't have fetched much on t'market,
That's true, but our good name were kept inside it.
Rudd, Rudd, a lovely name, Rudd, your dad's name,
A name we carried proudly. Now it's smashed,
And we're disgraced in the eyes of all Skipton.
Evil news is shouted to t' rooks
But good is only whispered to t' snails.
That's why we're here, to fight the whiffle-whaffle.
So no more talk of getting my jug repaired.
The only craftsman I'll pay brass to is one
Who'll build stocks to shove that dulbert there inside
Or else a stake we can watch him burning at
While our name blazes from t'ashes pure and white.

SCENE 4

Adam enters

Martha Now then, judge Adam.
Tommy   Now then.
Leslie   Now then.
Eve   Now then.
Let's drop t'case, Mam.
Adam   What's brought this lot, brainbox?
Bright Nowt much. Some fuss over a cracked pot.
Adam Fathead, I hold you responsible for this.
A cracked pot! Couldn't you have got rid of them?
Can't we have summat more dignified
Today of all days? Have you no nous, lad?

Here's Judge Walter, all t'way from Manchester,
Who thinks Skipton the back of beyond to start with,
And what's he find but a flock of sheep-shaggers
Thumping and fratching over a crocked crock.
You did this on purpose to embarrass me.

Bright Me?

Adam   Yes, you, thruster, don't come the innocent.
(*to Eve*) Eve, just one word. Why's everyone here?

Eve What?

Adam   Why's everyone here?
(*to Bright*) Brainbox, I'm not sure I can take this case.
It's demeaning, I've no wig, and I feel ill.

Bright If Judge Clegg doesn't object, sir, I suppose
I could step in and...

Adam   Weasel. (*To Eve*) Eve, in the name of God
Will you tell me what it is that's brought you.
Is it that jug?

Eve   Yes.

Adam   Nowt else?

Eve   No.

Adam Are you sure?

Eve   Yes. Good. Silent as stones.

Walter Judge Adam, time's getting on, can we begin now?

Adam What's that? (*To Eve*) You know what I keep in my trousers.

Walter I said: Come and sit down and let's get on.

Bright Judge Adam, are you...?

Adam   Me? Why pick on me?

Bright   What?

Walter You seem preoccupied. Is anything wrong?

Adam You're right, m'lud, I am a bit. It's my cock,
It's wilting, I'm very worried about it,
My bantam cock. I bought it from a fellah
Just back from t'Punjab—he runs t' grocery.
Now it's got t' pip, and it's getting on my pip, too.
I was just getting advice from this young lady.
My little birds, my little chuck-chucks,
I'm an old softie, sir, I dote on them.

Walter All right, but you must now call the plaintiffs
And cross-examine them.

Adam   Fine. Would his lordship
   Like the case to be conducted formally
   Or according to our way in Skipton?
Walter In accordance with the standard procedures,
   Which are yours in Skipton, too, I'm sure.
Adam Fine, fine, you want it formal, I get it.
   Nowt for it, then: things'll break or bend, soon see.
   Are you ready Mr Bright?
Bright   Ready, sir.
Adam Is your nib dipped? Have you fresh paper?
Bright   Yes, sir.
Adam May all good men and true, and from Lancashire,
   In God's name witness that justice be done. Amen.
   Step forward, everyone. This here's Judge Walter.
Leslie   ⎫
Martha   ⎪
Tommy   ⎬ (*together*) Now then.
Eve   ⎭
Adam   From Manchester.
Leslie   ⎫
Martha   ⎪
Tommy   ⎬ (*together*)   Manchester!
Eve   ⎭
Adam Aye, Manchester, no need to goggle.
   He's keeping an eye on us, that's all,
   To make sure we do things right. So you just mind
   You're civil. Right, who's t' plaintiff?
Martha   Here I am, sir.
Adam Who are you?
Martha   Who?
Adam   You.
Martha   Who am I?
Adam   Yes, who, you?
   Name, position and place of residence.
Martha Go on, tha's mucking me about, sir.
Adam Mucking you about? I'm here to exercise
   The law, Mrs Rudd, and the law must know
   Your name.
Martha   Tha's known me while twenty-five year.

Tha knew my poor late husband, tha knows my Eve,
Tha passes my door every Sunday on thy walk.
Walter Can I safely infer you know this woman?
Adam She lives just round t'corner, your lordship,
A midwife, and t'widow of a gamekeeper,
An honest woman, decent, name of Rudd.
Walter May I suggest, Judge Adam, since you appear
So exceedingly well-informed about her,
Your inquisition's a touch superfluous.
Simply record the name of this good woman
And write alongside: "well known to the court".
Adam Fine, fine, by all means. You're not such a stickler
For formalities as I'd thought. Mr Bright,
Do as his lordship says: "well known to the court".
Walter Now can we establish the plaintiff's object.
Adam Her object?
Walter   What is her object in coming here?
Adam Oh, I know what her object is—a pot.
Walter A pot? How do you know that?
Adam   Aye, a pot.
A plain, ordinary pot. Put pot, Bright,
And write alongside: "well known to the court".
Bright Sir, I were only speculating earlier.
Mrs Rudd hasn't actually said yet that...
Adam Look, when I tell you to write summat down
You write it, right, Bright? In't it a pot
Mrs Rudd?
Martha   Yes, a jug.
Adam   See!
Martha   A broken one.
Adam And who broke it, eh? That there lout, were it?
Martha Aye, that there lout, that lout there.
Adam   That'll do me.
Accused well known to the court. End of case.
Leslie It's not true, sir. She's lying through her teeth.
Adam Silence. You can have your say from t'stocks.
Write down "pot", Mr Bright, as I said before,
Then "broken" beside it, and then the name
Of the accused. Now we'll prove his guilt.

Walter Judge Adam, whoah, you're racing ahead.

Adam Surely not.

Bright   We must observe formalities.

Adam Formalities? No, brainbox, you're wrong there.
  His lordship doesn't hold with formalities.

Walter Judge Adam, if you've not already grasped
  The principles of conducting a court case...

Adam Forgive me, I must have misheard. I swear you said
  We weren't standing on ceremony.

Walter   What I said
  Was I expect you to dispense justice,
  And I assume the law here in Skipton
  Is the same as throughout the West Riding.

Adam There I must take issue, m'lud. We have here
  In Skipton our own unique traditions
  Honed like a scythe through each generation.
  Now from these I've departed not a jot.
  But if you want me to run things different, that's fine,
  I'm easy, whichever way you deem best—
  I'll try t'Manchester way if you insist.

Walter I'm not sure we're understanding each other.
  Never mind: you had better start again.

Adam Don't worry, m'lud. There's a slow meandering way
  To justice, through t'valleys, and a fast climb,
  Using local sheep-paths over t'hills: either road,
  You'll find they take us both to t'same place.
  Mrs Rudd, please now tell us your complaint.

Martha Dost tha see this jug, your honours, dost tha?

Adam Yes, yes, we see it.

Martha   Nay, begging thy pardon,
  Tha don't begin to, all tha sees is t'bits.
  T'prettiest pot that ever lived has passed away,
  A jug that were like a honey-fall to me.
  See this piece here? That's where history began.

Adam T'garden of Eden?

Martha   Nay, deeper roots than that:
  I mean t'wars of York and Lancaster.
  I mean a garden in London where Richard,
  Duke of York, plucked a white rose off a bush

And t'whole lot started, as depicted on my jug.
See, here's Richard's left foot, severed from his leg.
And here stood t'red rose mob of Lancaster:
Gone now, not a sword or stocking left of 'em,
As though t'wind had blown their rosebuds all to nowt.
On t'next bit is t'battle Richard died at
Near Wakefield; right here is t'mound of dung
You (*to Walter*) Lancashire hooligans stood him on,
And here's Queen Margaret snarling like a she-wolf
As she sticks a paper crown over his head.
His head's off now...

Walter   It was off then, soon enough.

Martha On my jug it were still sitting firmly
On his shoulders, so you saw his look of shock
As a red rose soldier caught up with his young son
And thrust a coward's dagger in his back.

Walter That soldier was Lord Clifford—from Skipton.
You see your history through rose-hued lenses.

Martha You and all, your lordship. There's always turncoats
That fight on t'wrong side. Look at this pot-lug:
Two Yorkists killed at once: such a piteous scene
T' painter of my jug has added on t' handle
Grown men carrying buckets full of tears.
You can't see t'buckets now, nor nowt else neither:
It's me should be brushing my tears away
Now all this jug's history's been wiped out.

Walter Enough tears now, Mrs Rudd. No more harping
On the ancient past. You must continue.

Martha Continue? Aye, t'line continued here, see,
With Edward, Richard's other son, at Towton,
When snow blew in t'faces of Lancaster
And t'Yorkists come down on 'em like a dog-pack
And t'river Wharfe ran crimson with their blood.
Weheh, one for t'Tykes. But look, not even t'head
Of Ted's been left, nor nowt of t'next battle,
Barnet—another one to t'Whites—and *this*
Is t'sum of Tewkesbury, when old Margaret
Were carted off to t'Tower after t'lads ran rampant
Yet again. Three-one to us. T'last scene's Bosworth.

You can see King Richard wi' his crook-back,
And his crown rolling under a hawthorn,
And t'sword of Henry Tudor buried up to t'hilt
In his poor heart. Look at him now. Deformed?
I'll say King Richard's deformed all right,
E's nowt but a crammly leg and withered arm,
And 'is shadow leaking blood over t'hayfield,
And 'is horse buggered off to kingdom come.
T'most tragic noble history of our county
And t'parlous evil of Lancaster
—All gone now, smashed to bits and turned to nowt.

Walter Please no more muddled history lessons,
Mrs Rudd. It's not the scenes on your jug
We want to hear about, but who broke it.

Martha I'm getting to that, sir. But I must tell thee
Of t'birth of my jug first, and its young years.
It were made in Stoke in seventeen hundred
For a duke who gave it to his duchess.
But it fell into t'hands of a tinker
Who'd come flogging knick-knacks at t'great house
And had his wicked way with a chambermaid
And stole this precious pot as he cleared off.
Now this tinker were a braggart: wherever
He went he liked to show off his booty
And at a fair in Hellifield one Whitsun
It were stolen from his knapsack while he slept…

Walter Could you get her to come to the point Judge Adam?

Adam Now Mrs Rudd…

Martha   Next time t'jug were heard of
Were in Grassington, at t'home of a gravedigger
Called Clodd. A sober chap he were, who used it
Only three times in his life—t'first occasion
Were at sixty when he wedded a young wench;
T'second when she made him a proud daddy;
T' third time were fifteen children later
When t'poor lass died of sheer exhaustion
And Clodd led off wi' t'singing at her wake…

Adam Good, good, that's a nice little tale, but…

Martha T'next to own my jug were called Ramsbottom,

A weaver from Keighley who scrimped and scramped
And set himself up with a spinning jenny
Which folk said would do them out of work.
T'weaver were worried they'd smash up his machine,
And panicked one night when they were riding t'stang—
That's making a row to shame a wife-beater—
And hearing 'em coming chucked all he owned
Out of t'back window, then chucked himself out too
And broke his neck. My husband, passing by,
Heard him peg out. But t'jug, though made of clay,
He picked up from t'cobbles good as new.
Adam Remarkable.
Walter   But please get to the point.
Martha Here it comes. By t'time t'French were revolting...
Adam For God's sake, woman, are you not done yet?
There's a ducking stool for t'likes of you.
Martha Nay, if I can't state my case, Judge Adam,
It's useless my coming here and I'll be off
And find another judge who'll listen.
Walter Of course you have a right to state your case.
But you must stick to the point. If you're saying
The jug was worth a lot to you, well, fine,
That's all we need to know.
Martha   What tha needs to know
I'm not rightly clear. All I know is my jug's broke.
Walter Right. So let's come to that. Your husband got it.
What happened to the jug next?
Martha   That's just my point—
Nowt happened to t'jug, there weren't even a scratch on it
In t'fire that razed our house down ten year since.
When I pulled t'jug out of t'ashes next day,
Its glaze were still unbroken as a virgin
As if I'd taken it fresh-baked out of t'kiln.
Walter Good. Now we're fully acquainted with the jug.
Now we know all that has happened to it
And all that hasn't. Now we know its lineage,
Its social standing, its political views,
Which school it went to, its religion,
The identity of the potter who made it,

The colour of the smock he wore that day,
The heat of his kiln. Is there anything more?

Martha You bet your white wig there's more. Look at it.
A jug that were once fit for a duchess,
That even t'lips of a queen of England
Could have drunk from—that jug's smashed to figments.
And that bastard smirking in his shoes smashed it.

Adam You mean Leslie Dixon.

Martha   I do.

Leslie   She's lying, sir.

Adam You shut your trap until I open it.
Have you got that down, Mr Bright?

Bright   Yes, sir.

Adam So proceed, my dear, honest Mrs Rudd.

Martha It's about eleven last night, see.
I'm in bed and about to snuff my candle
When I damn near yanked clean out of my wits.
There's voices, a right rumpus it is,
Coming from t'next room, my daughter's bedroom.
It's like t'Devil himself is burgling us.
I shoots through like a flitbat out of hell
And what do I find? Her door broken open,
Someone stood there cussing and beldering,
And my jug on t'floor in tiny splinters.
Eve's wraithly-pale while that hulking rantipole
Looks red in t'face with guilt. I sift through t'bits
Like they were tea-leaves and their message
Stares me in t'face: he's a filthy tit-chaser,
It were my daughter's jugs he were after,
She fought him off and he broke my jug instead.

Adam Sounds very convincing to me.

Walter   Continue.

Martha What the hell's he doing here so late,
I ask him, charging round in t'dead of t'night
Smashing up folks' pottery. And what's he say,
The gowky sod, the great idle clod of clay?
He says someone else did it, someone else
Were in t'bedroom before him and did a bunk.
And all t'while he's laying into my lass,

Calling her tart and shagbag and buer,
Gammerstang, lad-louper, flappysket and whore,
And says even t'bed sheets reek of her mischief.
When he's stopped ranting I turn to my Eve
Who's stood there pale as a boggart and I say:
Is what he's saying right? God in heaven,
She says—she's sat down on t' bed now, crying—
What do you take me for, Mam? So it were him,
Says I. Who else, says she, and then she swears it.
Eve What did I swear, what? I swore nowt to you.
Martha Eve!
Eve   It's not true, Mam.
Leslie   Now maybe tha'll listen.
Adam Shut your gob, you ugly Tyke. This is where
You'll be going. (*He opens the trapdoor*) We'll deal with you later.
Martha So you're saying now you didn't...
Eve   Swear, no.
You made that up, Mam. It twists my guts
To go against you in here, but I swore nowt.
Adam Now ladies, don't get so worked up.
Bright   Strange, that.
Martha So what tha's saying is tha didn't swear
By Almighty God...
Eve   That's right, I didn't.
And to that I will swear by Almighty God.
Adam Hey! hey, ladies, enough of this thratching.
Mrs Rudd, you're frightening t'poor child.
She's waffly as a mill-sail. Let her think on
And then she'll soon remember what she said
About what happened, not what will happen
If she says t'wrong thing in a sacred courtroom
And ends up being jailed for perjury.
Walter Whoaah, Judge Adam, you'll intimidate her
More than her mother's doing with threats like that.
Martha If she's got t'nerve, that shameless hussy,
To tell me to my face that someone else,
Not her betrothed, were in her bedroom...
All right, I don't know for sure if she swore it,
But I know she said it, I swear she did.

Adam That's right, and I've no doubt she'll say it now,
 Won't you, Eve?

Martha   Out with it, lass. Come on, cough up.

Eve I don't deny that's what I said.

Adam   There you are.

Leslie The lying slag…

Adam   Write it down, Bright.
 Conclusive evidence against the accused.

Tommy   Shame on her.
 She's telling more stories than I have sheep.
 Next thing she'll be saying it were t'clerk there.

Walter Mr Bright, what you'll put in the records,
 I hope, is simply what the girl has admitted
 She said last night—not that a certain person
 Is guilty, which still remains to be proved.
 Isn't it now her turn to be a witness?

Adam My word, yes, and if it isn't her turn
 Then t' law's an ass and I've hairy ears.
 On the other hand, since she's t' youngest,
 Maybe I should question t' accused first?
 You're the inspector—whatever you say.

Walter Here's what I say. Get a grip. Be decisive.
 Frankly your handling of this case baffles me.

Adam Forgive me, my mind's not on the job, I know.
 I keep thinking of that sick bird of mine,
 My bantam, and of his favourite hen,
 His little chickadee, her warmth, her sweet breast.
 If only she'd swallow my medicine.
 Apologies, m'lud, I'll concentrate now.
 Accused, step forward.

Leslie   Here, sir, Leslie Dixon!
 Son of Tommy Dixon, a farm-hand from Carleton.

Adam Now am I right in supposing that you've heard
 Mrs Rudd's accusation against you?

Leslie   Aye.

Adam And have you summat, dare you say summat
 Against what's been alleged? Will you confess
 Or do you presume to defy God himself
 And deny the crime?

Leslie   Too true I deny it.
Too true I've summat to say in my defence.
There isn't a scrap of truth in what she's said.
Adam Very well—so you claim. And can you prove it?
Leslie Oh aye, I can prove it.
Adam   Now Mrs Rudd,
Don't fret yourself, I'll see you right, don't worry.
Walter Judge Adam, impartiality, please.
What's this concern for Mrs Rudd?
Adam   Concern?
She's upset, m'lud, and as a Christian I...
Walter Accused, go ahead and state your evidence.
Adam Well, Dixon. Spit it out, lad. Don't just stand there
Gawping like a heifer. We're waiting, man.
Come on. Where's your submission?
Leslie Summat like nine-thirty last night, it were,
Right warm, too, more like August than March.
I says to Dad, Dad I says, I'll just scuttle
Round to Eve's. Me and her, we're to be wed, like.
A right fit lass she is, as tha sees.
Walter   Fit?
You mean healthy?
Leslie   You know, a corker, bonny.
But strapping, too: tha should see her at harvest,
She's stronger at lifting bales than lads I know,
A dab hand, fast, too, nifty as a field-mouse.
We've been walking out nigh on a year now,
Since she gave t'lad she were with t'go-by.
It were last harvest, after t'mell supper,
In t'fog-field, I popped t'question.
How about it, I says, you and me, tied,
Us two, betrothed. Don't talk daft, she says:
You think I fancy being a farmer's wife?
Why not, I says, my mam was, till she died,
It's not a bad life. Not my life, she says.
But later she says yes.
Adam   Stick to t'point, lad.
I says and he says and she says—I ask you.
Leslie But she did say yes, Judge Adam, honest.

Walter Proceed.

Leslie   I says: Are you deaf, Dad. Can't I go?
We'll nobbut be yapping a while at t'window.
Get on with thee, then, says he, but mind tha stays
Outside her house. Right enough, word of honour,
Says I. Be off then, says he, but don't be late.

Adam Says he, says she, says I, says everyone:
Haven't you run out of sayings by now?

Leslie So I puts my cap on, and my coat and clogs,
And because t'beck's near bursting its banks
I take t'path through t'meadow round t'back of.t'great house.
But t'fields are boggy, or blathry with muckspreading,
And it takes a good while, and halfway there
I suddenly thinks to myself: you're sunk,
Leslie, you've made a bollocks, you're in t'shit:
T'back gate at Martha's will be locked by now:
T'old dragon won't leave it open after ten,
So if I'm not there by ten I'm not coming.

Adam The way these young uns do their courting now...

Walter And then?

Leslie   Well, I plough on any road,
And just as I gets there, where t'chestnut trees
Sort of splaudy up like t'tower of t'parish church,
Just then I hears t'back gate creaking, and I think:
Eh up, grand, t'lass is still waiting for me.
And I peers through t'dark to see if my eyes
Can catch t'same message my ears are picking up
When, Christ, I can't believe my own peepers,
I'm blind, I think, better take a second look,
I send 'em out on drill again, like sentries,
Only this time I have to give my eyes
A right good telling off: what they're picking up's
T'worst sort of slander. I gives 'em one last chance:
I tell myself they're doing their duty,
That's all, and if you keep putting them through it
Like this they'll be popping out of thy head next
And buggering off to work for someone else.
Cos they can't like what they see: it's Eve,
My eyes have nabbed her with another man.

Adam Oh yes, another man: *who,* cleverhead?
Leslie Who? Aye, by God you're asking me one there...
Adam If you can't name him, then we can't blame him.
Walter Go on. Proceed with your testimony.
Leslie I couldn't swear on t'Bible who it were.
It were pitch-black, tha sees, if tha could see,
Which I couldn't. But I'll tell thee this for nowt:
A butcher's lad, name of Wesley Higson,
Has been sniffing round my Eve for some time.
A right greasehorn he is, clarting all over her.
I told her last backend: Eve, I told her,
I'll not have that jolthead hanging round thy skirts,
He's slavering like you were a pot roast.
If you don't send him packing, I'll duff him over.
Well, she did tell him, after a fashion.
But he's still been hanging round like cured ham
From t'ceiling.
Adam   And this man's name is Higson?
Leslie Aye.
Adam   Good, it's a name. We'll soon find out more.
Higson. Have you noted that down, Mr Bright?
Bright Oh yes, and a good bit besides, sir.
It's surprising, the evidence I've noted.
Adam Leslie, good lad. Now set yourself at ease
And go on with your story. We're listening.
Leslie Through t'dark I sees t'pair of them together,
Their heads melted into one, whispering, plotting
And canoodling. My blood begins to boil:
My little Eve consorting with t'Devil!
He's got horns and now I'm sprouting them too.
So I creeps nearer, right up by t'backyard gate,
And hides myself behind a rosebush,
Till I hears a giggle, then a tugging sound,
My God, it sounds as if they're going to...
Eve No! It's evil of you to say such things.
Leslie Aye, and it were evil of you to do 'em.
Martha (*to Leslie*) Just wait till I get thee on my own,
In a dark snicket one of these midnights...
Leslie Lovey and dovey it goes, on and on,

Sucky and mucky, fumbling and tumbling.
I thinks: You only get this after a wedding,
Usually, but there's not been one today.
Then next thing they're off in t'house, to her room,
Without so much as a vicar's say-so.

Martha You slandering ragabash. I'll warm thy jacket
For thee, I'll have thy bollocks for bookends.

Eve Leave off, Mam, I don't even care any more.
Let him have his say, then I'll have mine.

Adam You'll keep quiet. You'll wait till I call you
And if I don't call you, you'll not say a word.

Walter My God, this case gets stranger by the minute.

Leslie By now there's smoke coming out of my ears.
I'm choking and bursting a blood vessel.
Help, air! Buttons shoot off my waistcoat.
Help, air! I'm tearing my collar open.
I burst through t'gate, crash through t'door, belt upstairs
And thunder against her bedroom. T'door's bolted,
But I shove my foot against it and—crash—
I'm in: welcome to hell.

Adam   You impulsive lad.

Leslie As I enter, there's a clatter as t'jug falls
Off t'mantelpiece on to t'floor. And there he goes,
Yer man, t'Devil himself, with his forked tail
Or his coat tails flying behind.

Adam   Higson?

Leslie Who else could it have been? Eve's stood there.
I push her aside in a heap and hurry
To t'window. And there he is, just below,
T'bugger's got himself impaled on t'trellis,
He's dangling there like a great black grape on t'vine.
I find I've still got hold of t'door-handle,
I must have wrenched it off while forcing t'door—
Here, see, a good pound's weight of metal on it—
So I lean out and skelp him one on t'nut,
But he's still stuck so I welt him again,
Just to help him on his way, like.

Adam   A handle.

Leslie What?

Adam   From t'door.
Leslie   Aye, that's it, a door-handle.
Bright Ah, yes, that would explain it. Were you holding
  This end or that end?
Leslie   I were holding this end
  And I clunked him with that.
Adam   Very painful.
Bright Interesting, I'd worked out it must be
  A heavy object—that much was obvious.
Walter Let's get back to the case, gentlemen, please.
Adam Yes, don't get stuck in irrelevant detail,
  Brainbox. (*To Leslie*) Proceed.
Leslie   Thunk, t'bloke crashes below,
  He's ligging down and rigged like a sheep,
  It's silent as t'grave and I think he's croaked.
  I'm getting on t'sill to jump down after him
  When I hears him dragging himself up off t'ground.
  Still in t'land of living are you? Not for long.
  I'm stood on t'windowsill, ready to leap,
  When he chucks a handful of sand and grit
  Up into my chops—it stings like hailstones,
  And then him and t'night and t'window and all t'lot
  Collapse on top of me like a tent,
  I can't see nowt, lights go out on t'world.
Adam So who did that? Higson?
Leslie   It must have been.
Adam A cunning sod.
Bright   Yes, if it was him.
Adam   Who else?
Leslie Now it's my turn to plummet through t'air.
  Only backwards, into t'room, not out of it,
  Tipple-tail, like a rock-fall on to t'floor
  And nearly right through. Quick check. Neck broken?
  No. Backbone? No. Legs? Arms? All in order.
Adam Except those scratches, eh?
Leslie   That were t'grit.
Adam And that cut on your forehead?
Leslie   When I hit t'floor.
Adam A bloody good shot, whoever threw t'sand.

Leslie In t'meantime, t'jailbird has gone, t'bird in hand
Has flown, and I'm sat there wiping my eyes.
Then *she* pipes up, "Oh, Leslie, you're injured".
I pull my fist back to smack her one in t'gob,
I lift my leg to give her t'length of my foot,
But I can't see right, and I think: "Why waste my strength?"
So I call her a dirty nazz-moll instead.
But then my voice gets blocked with tears, see,
Then Martha waltzes in holding her candle
And I see Eve's shivering and pale as limestone.
So that's what doing it does to women,
I think, and it's like my gold has turned to ash.
Aye, there are worse things in life than being blind.
If anyone had asked me for my eyes, then,
To use for conker-fights, they could have had them.

Eve You're so cruel, you don't deserve the truth.

Adam   Silence!

Leslie You can guess all t'rest. Martha started foaming,
And skirling to t'heavens like a curlew,
And Dick and Ned came in, that's next-door neighbours
Either side, then aunt Betty, then aunt Bridget,
And school brats and peddlers and dogs and cats
And t'late shift coming back from Garforth's Mill,
T'whole damn rafflepack, just to gawp at us.
Then Martha screams "Who's cracked my pot?",
And she—her—Eve—said I'd done it, as tha knows,
And perhaps she weren't so far wrong, neither.
Cos there's one thing I did make a hole in—
The ugly great mug of that butcher's lad.

Adam Excellent. Well, that seems to wrap it up.

Walter Mrs Rudd, have you anything to add?
Speak up.

Martha   I'll tell you what I have to add.
That he's about as much respect for t'truth
As a fox has for chickens. Aye, he's a fox
All right, a thieving creature out of t'night.
He should be slung in t'stocks and clubbed to death.

Walter But you must produce some proof against him.

Martha I can. Here is my witness—my daughter.

Adam Your daughter? I'm afraid that's not possible.
Walter But why not?
Adam   As a witness, your lordship?
Walter Of course as a witness. Her evidence
   Could settle the case.
Adam   But sir, as a witness...
Walter Mr Bright, I take it that you're familiar
   With how to conduct a trial.
Bright   Me? Oh yes, sir...
Adam But it's in the statute books, isn't it,
   "In cases pertaining to domestic fracas",
   Some such phrase, "the plaintiff is not allowed
   To call on members of his own family,
   Who are deemed to be interested parties".
Walter Interested parties?
Adam   Yes, yes, it's coming back.
   Hodge versus Hodge, seventeen fifty-one,
   Divorce proceedings, t' wife alleged cruelty,
   Certain items had been thrown at her
   By her husband—a clock, a dinner service—
   And her counsel wished to call t' daughter
   As a witness, but she being t' sole heir
   And beneficiary, my learned sir refused.
   I'm sure I'm right. We could look it up.
Walter That brain of yours is an odd porridge.
   Yes, it could be that there was such a case.
   But we've not reached the High Court yet, have we?
   The girl would make an informal statement,
   That's all.
Adam   Only informal. I see.
   In Chichester I think it was, that Hodge case,
   If you'd like to check up on t' precedents...
Walter Step forward, child.
Adam   Hey, Meg, refreshments, please!
   Meg! I'm parched from all these testimonies.

Meg enters

A glass of ale, Meg.

Meg   Yes, sir.
Adam   And for you...?
Walter Nothing, thanks.
Adam   Some home-brew? Or wine? Just say.

Walter shakes his head

> *Meg exits. She re-enters and re-exits, silently delivering a glass of ale*
> *to Adam, during the following dialogue*

To be candid, m'lud, I think this case
Could be quickly settled by a compromise.
Walter A compromise? There you have me, Judge Adam.
Reasonable people can reach a compromise,
But I fail to see how one can be reached here
Among such intemperate wrangling
And with so much left to be untangled still.
Don't tell me you've already reached a verdict.
Adam When the law itself leaves me in t'dark,
I trust my instincts, my Craven kenning,
My feel for t'ways of folks who bide in Skipton.
Now, picking my way through t'evidence,
My nous tells me it must have been young Higson...
Walter Who?
Adam   Or Dixon.
Walter   What?
Adam   Or there again, Higson.
Walter Yes, well, which of them? Higson or Dixon?
The law's not a bran-tub. You can't just take pot luck.
Adam But mightn't they *both* be guilty of breaking t'jug?
We've established there were two men in t'room,
And who's to say this wasn't a joint burglary
That went wrong, with Dixon here shifting t'blame
On to his accomplice. Hard to stand up,
But that's t' compromise I meant, m'lud.
This is nobbut a domestic squabble.
At least this road we'd put an end to it.
Walter Just keep up the questioning: all will come out.
Adam Have it your way. Waste of time, but here goes.

Now Mr Bright, are you ready again?
Bright That I am. I've a fresh page to start on
And I can't wait to get something down on it.
Adam A clean sheet, eh? Fine.
Walter   Speak up now, my child.
Adam If I can just set her at ease, your lordship.
(*Aside to Eve*)
You've not forgotten what I keep in my keks?
There are all sorts of death—by sword, gun, fever,
Could be yellow, could be red, take your pick.
Walter Please curtail the briefing—time's getting on.
Adam (*aside*) Hear it crumpling? Do you want him crumpled, too?
Walter Judge Adam, did you hear me? We must proceed.
Adam I'm merely trying to soothe her nerves, m'lud.
Walter Well, do it in front of the court. She's young,
I know, but she doesn't need pampering.
Adam I'm not a man of high polish, your lordship.
People from London may think me untutored
And people from Manchester find me slow.
But I know how to talk to folk from round here,
I speak their language and I tease t'answers
Out of them like trout from under a stone.
Walter All right. But isn't she now ready to speak?
Adam I think she is. I've been advising her
She must speak only t'truth in front of God,
And not upset his honour by burbling on
About things that have no bearing on t'case.
A judge has certain powers and influence.
You can never tell when you're going to need him.
Walter Good. Now she's absorbed that, she must address us.
Tommy Aye, get on, lass, no more messing about.
Some of us have brass to earn. Cough it up.
Leslie No way, Dad. It's not easy to cough up
When guilt's stuck like a fish bone in tha gullet.
Martha Keep your nose out. Come on Eve, who was it?
Eve Jesus.
Martha No, it weren't Jesus, you little minx.
Walter Mrs Rudd, I don't think she…
Martha   I'll tell thee this,

I'm glad her father's not here to see her now.
Just before he died, he says to me, "Martha,
Fix our kid up with a good man and I'll rest
In peace. But if she turns out a wrong un
You'd better pay t'gravedigger to roll me
On my back again, for I'll have turned in t'grave
And worms of shame'll be nibbling my face."

Adam Mrs Rudd, please, give t'poor girl a chance.
Don't frighten her. Let her just collect herself.

Leslie Collect herself, aye—they've all been collecting her.
Every lad in Skipton's had her in his album.
She'll have to start again in another town.
There's one up dales would suit her down to t'ground:
Hawes.

Adam   That's your last warning. (*He points to the trapdoor*) Down here
next time.

Leslie Nay, no need, I've had my say now, no sweat:
It'll be my name she comes up with, I bet.

Eve You could have said it was you, if you love me.
If only you'd said, "Fine, fair dos, I broke t'pot",
That would have been that, and we'd not be here.
I'm ashamed of you, Leslie, really ashamed.
Can't you trust me? Didn't I give you my hand?
Have you ever had reason to doubt me?
You know that slobby butcher lad's no rival.
Just suppose you had looked through t'keyhole
And seen me in my room with another man,
Shouldn't you still have thought: Eve's reliable,
I know she'll have an explanation for this,
And if I don't get it in this life I'll save
My questioning till t'next world, beyond t'grave.

Leslie T'next life's too long for me to wait, Evie.
I'm a simple soul—I believe my own eyes.

Eve Let's suppose I was with Higson last night.
But let's suppose, too, I had my reasons
For keeping it from my mam and t'neighbours:
Well, then, why shouldn't I say it was you
Who'd been with me, Leslie? Why shouldn't l?—

Leslie You can say what the fucking hell you think—

Say me, if you want me to end up in t'clink.
Eve Maybe you do deserve to end up there.
Maybe I've been stupid trying to save you...
Leslie Save me!
Eve   Yes, from summat worse. One word from me
Could clear my name but ruin you for good.
Walter What is this word, dear? *Wasn't* it Leslie?

Pause

Eve No, your honour, since it's what he wants to hear,
And I only kept mum for his sake any road:
Leslie didn't break Mam's jug, that's official.
Martha So you were lying to me?
Eve   Sorry, Mam, aye.
I lied to stop summat worse happening.
Martha Here's worse: you're due for a nauping, my girl.
Where's my strap?
Eve   Lash all you like—it's nowt to me.
Walter Mrs Rudd, control yourself in court.
Adam I'll have her turfed out, the daft old bat.
Why should it have been Leslie, not Wesley?
Who knows, she might have cracked her own pot.
Martha Was it Wesley, was it?
Adam   Speak up, Evie, my sweet:
Wesley? Wesley?
Eve   You shameless old magpie!
You have the nerve, you, to accuse Higson when...
Walter Shh, young lady, shh, is that the respect
A judge deserves?
Eve   You what? Respect? Judge Adam?
Him who knows t'truth better than anyone.
Bright What's that the witness is saying exactly?
I have my pen ready. Please go on, Eve.
Eve (*to Adam*) How could you even pretend it was Higson?
Wasn't it you yourself sent him out of town
Yesterday on an errand? Remember?
Sent him off to the army commissioners
In York with a list of recruits' names.

So how can you say him when you know he's in York?

Adam Where's that get us? Not Dixon, not Higson?
Who's that leave, then? I'm lost.

Leslie   I think t'lass is right.
I'd forgotten but she can't be lying
Because I met Higson myself, off to York
As she said, round eight in t'morning it were,
And he's such a slow, bow-legged bowdykite
At walking even if he scraped a lift
Off a cart he'd not have been back by ten at night.
Let's face it: some other bugger's guilty.

Adam What are you on about, you great muttonchops?
Bowlegs my arse!

Leslie   He has. He's walked with a limp
Since he were a nipper. He's one leg bent
Like a barrel-hoop. T'most he can manage
Is a sort of paddle.

Adam   Higson! Rubbish!
That bloke can show a clean pair of heels
To t'best of them. I've seen him out on t'moor.
A collie at the summit of its health
Would have to trot flat out to keep up with him.

Walter We must come back to the girl's testimony.
Let's hear what she says.

Adam   A private word, m'lud.
Frankly the girl won't be much use to us.

Walter Won't be much use? Why?

Adam   She's like a finch, so shy
And afeard she's only to *see* a beard
And she blushes down to t'roots of her hair.
Whatever she were put through in t' dark last night
She'd be too embarrassed to own up to
In daylight. To force it from her would be cruel.

Walter Aren't you being over-protective of her?

Adam There's no harm in admitting, your lordship,
Her late father were a good friend of mine.
His last words to me were: "Look after Eve".
Now if we agreed to let her step down,
Saving her from reddening and stammering,

It would be more than a kindness, m'lud,
I'd be doing my duty by her dad.
Walter Very thoughtful of you. I confess, though,
The case intrigues me more by the minute.
Let's get to the bottom of it. Don't be afraid,
My child: just tell us simply who broke the jug.
Nothing else that happened matters to this court.
No indiscretions will be held against you.
Eve Sir, please let me off saying any more.
God gave us mouths to shut as well as open,
And it's in His name I claim my right to silence.
As I said, Leslie did not break mam's jug,
And if you ask me to go and swear it
At a holy altar, fine then, I will do.
But as to t'rest of last night's goings-on,
I'm saying nowt. Just because my mam knits
Doesn't give her rights to every ball of wool
In t'house—and there's one thread I'll not give her.
It's not my own secret I'm keeping, mind,
But someone else's, and it's a secret
That's got nowt to do with my mam's pot.
Sooner or later I tell her all t'lot,
But not now in court, and she can't force me.
Adam Quite right, my dear, she's no right, right enough.
Which means her case will have to be chucked out,
But I can't see any objection to that.
Walter Mrs Rudd, do you have any objection?
Martha If I don't say owt straight off, that's because
Summat's stuck in my gizzard, I'm choked off,
I feel I've had a stroke and my tongue's withered.
Tommy |
Leslie | (*together*) No chance.
Martha   I've heard of folks perjuring themselves
So as to save their skins, but to lie in court
So's to *lose* your good name, that's a new one on me.
Look, if I'd gone into her room last night
And found another man there, I'd not be here
In t'first place, nor her. I'd have stopped at home,
And fetched all her gee-gaws and traps and sticks

And laid them on t'front step, and I'd have said:
"There you go, lass, you can set up home outdoors,
Air's nice and roomy, and there's no rent to pay,
And tha's used to laying down in t'dirt now,
And if life in t'open air doesn't suit thee
With thy long hair tha can always hang thisen."

Walter Calm yourself, please calm yourself, Mrs Rudd.

Martha She won't lift a finger to help me,
But I know without a shadow it were him. (*She points at Leslie*)
Aye, it's poor hedge that han't a bit of shelter.
I've no need to remind you, your honours,
There's a war on: Leslie's due to get called up,
I hear it's only t'last papers he's waiting for,
Then he'll be off to swear his oath in Ripon.
It's a hard life fighting Boney, and we know
Some soldiers are too mardy to scrap.
Now I'm not saying Leslie's a spunkless sheep,
But just suppose he comes to Eve and says:
This is t'last chance I've got to do a bunk,
How about running off wi' me? T'world's our oyster,
All we need's a bit of brass to keep us,
And tha's got t'keys to thy mam's shilling tin.
And she's maybe hesitant, and he's shouting,
And my lovely jug gets smashed during t'scraffle.
It were cunning on his part, and love on hers.

Leslie You caggy old cow—you're talking through your arse.
Keys to her shilling tin, sir? Fat chance of that.
She's as tight as a wet clothes-line, that one.
Brass? My arse. Eve's as much hope of getting that
As I have of being made a colonel.

Eve Him a deserter, Mam? Me a thief?

Walter Let's stick to the facts. It's proof that we need.

Martha Proof? Easy. I could have fetched a hundred tongues,
I could have set up a whole row of them,
Tongue on tongue, like a crop of runner beans,
Wagging in t'air and telling their stories,
If I'd thought that dirty-bottomed daudle
Would refuse me hers. All I need is Bridget—
Who's an aunt of his, and all—one word from her,

And Leslie's defence'll crack wide open.
Because Bridget heard 'em jabbering in t'street.

Leslie What's all this cack?

Tommy   Bridget?

Leslie   Heard me with Eve?

Martha At half ten. That's just before, as he admits,
A man were in t'room pawing and mauling her
And trying to break open her precious vessel.

Walter Mr Bright, Judge Adam, let's fetch this woman.

Leslie Have a heart, your honour. It's a barrel of lies.
It doesn't hold water.

Adam   You just wait, you wicked lad.
Bright, a job for you—we need aunt Bridget.

Tommy You hacking great swoddy. Now I can see what
Tha were playing at. I'll break every bone...

Leslie What's up, Dad?

Tommy   What's up is you've been pulling t'fleece
Over my eyes. Mischief needs nobbut t'sun
To ripen its fruit. Why didn't tha tell me t'truth?

Leslie Fuck a duckling, Dad, because it isn't t'truth.
If aunty says it is, then string me up.

Tommy Butter wouldn't murl in thy mouth, would it?
Never mind what you and her've been telling t'court,
You're hiding under t'same blanket together,
Aye, and probably not for t'first time, neither.
There's some kind of mucky secret between you.

Leslie Secret. Give over. Why's tha blacking me, dad?
Why's tha bensiling and blairing at me?
Stop talking in riddles. What're you on about?

Walter Perhaps you would like to make a statement,
Mr Dixon.

Tommy   A statement, your honour, me?
Nay, I'm only an humble moor-ender from t'dales
And I've no fancy words for holding forth.
Get up, milk t'cows, see my sheep up on t'tops,
Bank up my eggs, stack up my drystone walls,
Bit of hotpot for dinner, then out again,
Check my silage and my beetcrops and my hay,.
Herd t'cows back to t'milking shed, muck out t'shippon,

Greave my peat, mow my bracken, crop my lings,
I've nobbut this one life day after day,
And no wife since t' lass passed on ten year since,
And wi' all young uns off to work in towns
I've nobbut one farm-hand, my son and heir,
And nobbut one word of advice for folk,
"Never start ploughing on a Friday"
And "If tha keeps to t'heather tha'll not get bogged",
And there's nobbut one letter I've learnt to read,
That's D for Dixon I daub on t'fleeces
Of my flock. As for t'law, t'only law I know
Is if it doesn't rain today it will tomorrow.
A statement, me? Nay, I'm not one for blish-blashing
And tongue-scraping, not till I've reckoned folks up,
Summered them and wintered them and summered them
Again till I can tell a ha'penny head
From a farthing tail. Nay, tha can count more geese
On my pond than t'words I speak in a day.
But I've some words for Leslie, that I have.
Why did thee pack? Eh? Why did thee pack thy bag?
Eh? Why did thee pack thy things last night?

Leslie What things?

Tommy   Thy jacket, thy keks and shirt, thy vest
And socks and long johns, all t'lot of 'em
Bundled up like a tinker's ballpack.

Leslie   Why?
Cos I'm going off wi' t'lads on Saturday.

Tommy Going where? Out tarting?

Leslie   Leave off. Fishing,
That's what.

Tommy   Fishing for little duckies, eh?

Leslie No, fishing for trout up at Malham Tarn.
And I need t'gear cos we're kipping overnight.

Tommy Tha'd got thy bloody skates on then, an't thee?
Saturday's three days off: it's not like thee
To do owt for thisen afore tha needs to,
Unless tha were doing a bunk with t'lass.

Walter Do you have anything to say with a bearing
On the case?

Tommy   I don't know what bearings are

In Lancashire, maybe summat made in factories,
But it's t'bearing of my son that worries me.
Like I say, I'm saying nowt about t'pot,
I were at home when it were broke. I came here
Believing that lad of mine were innocent
And I hoped he'd be found so by t'court
And then at least his engagement could be off
And we'd get some of t'brass back on t'ring.
But this stuff from Mrs Rudd about Leslie
Running off, it's putting t'wind up me,
I'm sprouting white hairs, I've begun to doubt him.
If he's guilty, there'll be no need for t'stocks:
I'll break his bloody neck for him first.

Walter I think we need aunt Bridget's evidence first.
Mr Bright, weren't you going to fetch her?

Bright Yes, I'm just off, m'lud.

Adam   By all means,
But aren't you getting a bit ragged out, m'lud?
You've still my files and records to check.
What time's it now?

Bright   Just gone half past.

Adam   What, ten?

Bright No, eleven.

Adam   Good Lord, the time's gone mad.
It is nearly dinner-time. What do you want to do?

Walter I think we should...

Adam   Call it a day? Excellent.

Walter Hang on, no: I think we should continue.

Adam Fine, fine, all one to me. Only, if we stopped
We could sit down over a jug or two
And natter a bit and look over my accounts
And I promise you I could wrap this case up
Next session, dead easy, in half an hour,
In accordance with formal procedures.

Walter Well, why not do that now then?

Adam   Just as you want.
What's keeping you, brainbox? Off with you for t'aunt.

Bright exits

While we're waiting, if it suits his lordship,
Why don't we stretch our legs and get some air?

Walter Um, all right. What I've been meaning to ask was…

Adam And while we're at it, if you don't object,
Why not let t'others have a break, too,
Till aunt Bridget…

Walter   The witnesses?

Adam   All t'lot.

Walter Judge Adam, do you know what, on second thoughts
I think perhaps a drink would do me good.

Adam Now there's a man after my own heart. Hey,
Margaret. Things are looking up here. Meg!

Meg enters

Meg Here, sir!

Adam   Now, what would you care for? Off, you lot.
Cut your sticks, stir your stumps, push off, get lost.
Some wine? Some ale?

Walter   Some of your own brew, fine.

Adam Excellent. Go on, wait till I call you—out!

Walter No need for them to leave…

Adam   Off, I said! And Meg,
Let's have a spread for t'man, a right slap-up:
We need bread, butter, ham, pickled onion,
Topside of beef with horseradish, pigeon…

Walter Please, no need to go to so much trouble.

Adam Jugged hare, shepherd's pie, beetroot, mustard, taties,
Apple pie, rhubarb crumble—I've told you, out!
Fresh cream, Wensleydale, port to follow…
What're you lot doing still skulking about?
I've told you, we're having a break now, out!

CURTAIN

ACT II

SCENE 1

Adam and Walter at the table, Adam singing

Adam
"It's hard when folks can't find their work
Where they've been bred and born.
When I were young I allus thought
I'd bide among roots and corn.
But I've been forced to work in towns
So here's my litany:
From Hull and Halifax and Hell
Good Lord deliver me!"
Like the song says, I feel sorry for you,
M'lud, having to traipse all over t'shop
And not being able to stop here, in God's own dales.

Walter Judge Adam, I expect we don't have long
And there's something I wanted...

Adam Not long, m'lud?

Walter Till your clerk comes back with this aunt Bridget.

Adam Well, alas and alack, it's market day.
She'll be down by t'sheep pens at t'auction mart
Among t'ewes and t'tups, haggling and bartering,
So it might take a bit to extract her.
Like I say, I could postpone proceedings...

Walter Oh, he seems resourceful, your clerk. He'll be here
Sharpish, I'm sure. Better make that my last beer,
Judge Adam. Nothing more to eat, thanks—I'm full.

Adam Full! I'll not hear of it. Tha's fading away,
You must have some bellytimber, your lordship.
You're like two lats in a rabbit-skin.
Yorkshire bite, we call it. Go on, get trenching.

Walter No, really.

Adam   At least try the Wensleydale.
We know how to make a good crumbly cheese
Round here, none of your stiff English counties
Or your soggy French rubbish. Your good health.
No old peculiar brews for you, m'lud:
This here's Adam's ale, the name some use for water,
But my brew's made of sterner matter.
Nowt fancy, m'lud, but we do our best.
I know we've a terrible name for ourselves,
Us bachelors, but we're proud of us standing.
We're single, meaning we're not content
With just one woman, we like several at once.
We're choosy, and so won't choose a wife.
We're selfish, and don't replenish the species,
Not that we'd own up to any road. True,
Too true. But you can say this much for us:
If you're saddled with a wife and breadsnappers
Then you're short of money and peace and time
Whereas we bachelors can sit down with a friend
And eat and drink and talk between ourselves
As long as we like. Ah, the solitary life:
Much underrated.

Walter   What I've been wanting to ask
Is how you came by your injuries, Judge Adam.
That's a pretty nasty wound on your forehead.

Adam You're right, m'lud. I'm proud of this perfect glaze
But it's cracked today. More beer?

Walter   What happened?

Adam I fell.

Walter   Fell. I see. When was this, last night?

Adam No, at cockcrow, about half-five this morning,
Just as I were climbing out of bed, dawn,
T'usual hour for me to start my studies.

Walter Oh, and how did you manage to fall over?

Adam To tell t'truth, it were myself I tripped over.
I still can't fathom how it fell out,
But I slipped and slammed my head against t'fire.

Walter You fell backwards?

Adam   Aye, arse-end-up.

Walter   And forwards?
You've two cuts, one at the front, one at the back.
Adam Aye, and I don't know which one's hurting t'most.
Walter But how?
Adam   Easy. First I crack my forehead
On t'range, bang! That sends me flying arseways
On to t'floor, whoosh! And I clunk myself one
On t'back of t'bonce, pow! Will you have more ale?
Walter A pretty odd story. If you were married,
I'd incline to a different explanation.
Adam How come?
Walter   You're so scritched and scratched about,
I'd think she must have got her nails in you.
Adam Nay, tha'll not catch me getting batterfanged.
Walter Something else to be said for bachelordom, eh?
Adam Good pot-shot, sir. We're not averse to t'ladies,
But we don't let them stick their claws in us.
You know what they say, your lordship: them that weds
Where they don't love, love where they don't wed;
But us bachelors don't love or wed at all.
No, these scratches you see, some twigs for silkworms
Drying out on t'stove, it were them did t'damage.
But enough about me—m'lud, your good health!
Mine, too: at least I didn't fall in t'Strid.
You know t'verses, sir? A poet from up t'Lakes.

              "And hither is young Romilly come,
              And what may now forbid
              That he, perhaps for the hundredth time,
              Shall bound across the Strid?

              "He sprang in glee—for what cared he
              That the river was strong and the rocks were steep,
              But the greyhound in the leash hung back,
              And checked him in his leap.

              "The boy is in the arms of Wharf,
              And strangled by a merciless force.
              For never more was young Romilly seen
              Till he rose a lifeless corpse."

Got a nice roll to it, eh, your lordship?
Like I say, my tumble could have been worse.
Walter But you've been unlucky all the same,
What with your wig choosing today to go missing,
So you couldn't even cover your wounds.
Adam Aye, misfortune always comes in twos,
That's my view—double trouble, don't they say?
I expect they must mean marriage again, eh?
No disrespect, m'lud, if you've tied the knot.
Now then, what about a chunk of this?
Walter Only a tiny bit. Is that the Wensleydale?
Adam Aye, fetched straight down from Hawes only this morning.
Walter So how exactly did you manage it?
Adam Well, a farmer I know who has this pony
And trap…
Walter   I meant how did you lose both your wigs?
Adam Oh, that. I were sat studying my files
Last night, and because I've mislaid my specs
I'm bending right down into t'papers
And poring over them, as one does, you know,
Utterly immersed in some legal quandary,
A repugnant will or boundary dispute,
And t'finer points are snuffing out all else,
I'm rapt in thought. Next thing, my wig's alight,
Set blazing by t'candle I'm reading by.
Oops, God's caught up with this poor sinner at last,
I think, he's going to roast me alive.
I try to wrench t'wig off but it's tied, see,
And in a flash it's burning like Sodom
And Gomorrah. Knackt. Scorched black as a fireback.
Walter Nasty. And your second wig's in town, you say?
Adam Yes, at t'wigmakers. Now, this rhubarb crumble…
Walter You know, I've a horrible feeling
We'll not be able to solve this case today,
But I should have thought you, with your local knowledge,
Could identify the culprit by his wounds.
A harsh sentence would be unnecessary.
If I were sure no great injustice would ensue,
I'd happily leave things in your hands.

The court's dignity is my only concern.
Now have you something you'd like to share with me?
Adam (*after a pause*) Aye, this wine.
Walter   Elderflower? Or is it rhubarb?
Adam Elderflower. You've a good nose, haven't you.
Walter I'm famous in Manchester for my nose.
  I can sniff things. I sense when a case is off.
Adam A gift, m'lud.
Walter (*after a pause*) Have you nothing to tell me?
  (*He pauses*) Let's review the evidence then, shall we?
  Tell me, how high is Mrs Rudd's window?
Adam Which window?
Walter   The window of her daughter's room.
Adam It's upstairs, about twelve foot from t'ground,
  Didn't she say? More wine?
Walter   And dangerous to jump from
  Because of the vine below with its branches.
Adam I imagine. Sup up.
Walter   No, that's enough.
Adam   Go on, be bold.
Walter It's still half-full.
Adam   Half-empty, more like.
  Down t'gargoyle with it. Then let's be topping you up.
Walter So the culprit's face would be badly scratched...
Adam Now we must make up t'holy trinity.
  T'first bottle's darkness. T'second's purgatory.
  T'third bottle's God, who's in his heaven
  And all's right with t'world. Home-brewed ambrosia:
  Go on, m'lud, get that stuck across your chest.
  There, you'll be downing firmaments next.
Walter And how many times did young Dixon say
  He hit the intruder on the head?
Adam I forget. He were maybe lying, any road.
  Have you ever heard this one sung, m'lud?
  "Where wor ta bahn when aw saw thee, aw saw thee.
  On Il-il-kley Moo-or ba-ah t'hat..."
  Without a hat, that means...
Walter   Yes, bare-headed,
  Dixon said. But how many blows did he strike?

Adam How many times did he hit the boy?
   Or whip the boy? Or hit the whipping boy?
   Twice worn't it? Once, then one for t'road, eh?
Walter Front and back, he implied?
Adam   Front and back, dead hard.
Walter He could almost have killed the man, couldn't he?
Adam Killed? Dead right. You've hit t'nail in t'coffin, there.
   Why assume t'culprit is still living.
   He's probably laid out stone-cold, and no lying.
   We might be looking for a corpse on t'moors.
   "Then ducks'll come and eat up worms, eat up worms."
Walter And because it was dark, he didn't recognize
   The man he struck.
Adam   That's it, not a glimmer.
   He should've ate up his carrots and peeled his eyes.
   Rack it back!
Walter   But though he didn't see this man...
Adam Cos grit were thrown: serve him right for staring...
Walter ...the culprit could be identified by his wounds.

Pause

Adam Have you thought, your lordship, wi' his cuts and scabs
   Young Leslie must look like the man he clunked,
   Or said he did. Do you smell a rat? Cheers.
Walter Cheers. To justice, honour, goodness and truth.
Adam Right. Might as well finish t'dregs, your lordship.
Walter So we're looking for someone with a motive
   For visiting Mrs Rudd's house...
Adam   No doubt.
   And where might you be visiting next, sir?
Walter   Leeds.
Adam Leeds! You'd best keep your wits about you there.
   It's a parlous evil place, Leeds is.
                        "There was a man who lived in Leeds
                        He set his garden full of seeds
                        And when the seeds began to grow
                        It were like a garden full of snow
                        And when the snow began to melt

It were like a ship without a belt
And when the ship began to sail
It were like a bird without a tail
And when the bird began to fly
It were like a stormclap in the sky
And when the sky began to roar
It were like a lion at my door
And when the door began to crack
It were like a penknife in my back
And when my back began to bleed
I were dead, dead, dead indeed."

Walter Yes, very cheering. I expect you must call
At Mrs Rudd's.
Adam   Not often.
Walter   But why not?
Isn't she the widow of a good friend?
Didn't you promise to keep an eye on her daughter?
Adam That's as may be. I'm not often round there.
Walter You've not been falling out with her, have you,
A man of the people like you? Come on,
You can be straight with me. (*He pauses*) I'll ask her, then...
(*Calling out*) Mrs Rudd!

Martha enters

You've not been falling out with
Judge Adam? He says he doesn't drop in much.
Martha Your honour, I don't think we've fallen out.
The bettermy folk have their ways, and we've ours,
But Judge Adam's not one to put on airs.
He can always hang his hat up in my house,
And I'm sure he still calls himself a friend.
But I've nowt much to stir on next to some folks
And it's been several weeks since he were in.
Walter I'd got the impression he dropped by most Sundays.
Martha Now and then he's peered in at t'window
Or if we're outside passed t'time of day
With me and t'lass, but then he's been straight off.
Parson Blacklaw and his wife: now he calls there.

Walter But hasn't your daughter helped Judge Adam
  With his sick bantams or whatever they are?
  He told me she'd given him some advice.
Martha That's right enough, sir: round here at t'courthouse,
  Only yesterday, she looked at his cock,
  Had the dropsy it did, all pale and sickly,
  Even its purple crest that sticks up so fierce
  Had gone droopy. She thought it would croak, poor thing.
Walter (*confused*) Top me up again, will you, top me up:
  I don't think I understand this town of yours.
  We may as well have another.
Adam   Delighted!
Martha Now if I had some of that stuff you're supping
  Which my late husband were partial to as well,
  Maybe Judge Adam would come calling more.
  But I'm nobbut a poor widow on my tod,
  And there's nowt in my house to take his fancy.
Walter ⎤
                (*together*) Oh, I'm not sure about that, Ms Rudd.
Adam   ⎦

SCENE 2

Bright, aunt Bridget (with a wig in her hand), and the rest of the cast, enter

Tommy Now then, aunt Bridget.
Bridget   Now then.
All   Now then, now then, now then.
Bright This is Bridget Howker, your honour.
  Bridget, this is Judge Clegg, from Manchester.
Walter Mr Bright, why is the witness carrying a wig?
Bright (*deeply smarmy*) Your honour?
Walter   Why does the witness have a wig?
Bright If your honour will have a word with Judge Adam,
  I'm sure we'll find out who the wig belongs to.
Walter It's not who it belongs to I want to know
  But how she came to have it.
Bright   She found it.
  It was nestling in Mrs Rudd's trellis...

Bridget That's it, perched like a bird's nest in t'vine
It were...
Bright   ...Or like one of those balls of wool
That a sheep leaves behind on a bramble.
And it was right under the bedroom window
Where Mrs Rudd's daughter sleeps.
Martha   My trellis!
Walter (*aside*) Judge Adam, if you've anything at all
To disclose to me now in confidence,
I urge you to confess it. We've the good name
Of this court to think of.
Adam   Something to confess?
Walter Well, haven't you?
Adam   Not a henscrat, sir.
Walter Do you recognize this wig? Could it be yours?
Adam Rooks and jackdaws, I think you may be right.
Well, if it isn't the very peruke
I gave to that lad there a week ago,
Who was meant to take it to Harrogate.
Walter Who? What?
Bright   Dixon?
Tommy   Leslie?
Leslie   Me?
Adam   You idle sod,
Didn't I entrust the wig to you, eh,
When you were off to Harrogate a week ago?
Didn't I tell you to put it into t'hands
Of Beckwith the barber, for him to clean?
Leslie You give it me, aye.
Adam   So why didn't you do
As I instructed, you burgling bugger?
Leslie So why didn't I? Hell's hairpiece, I did.
I takes it to t'barbers, just like you said,
And Mr Beckwith takes it off me...
Adam   Yes,
And then yesterday he sneaks back to Skipton
And hangs it in the vine of your fiancé.
You mowdywarp, you don't get off so lightly.
There's summat putrid here, I can catch a whiff,

It smells like revolt, peasants' revolt, to me.
It smells like fancy French cheeses in our market,
And good old English customs being o'erthrown.
If you'd allow me to proceed, your honour,
I'd like to cross-examine this woman.

Walter You handed over the wig?

Adam   Your lordship,
Before that lad there went off to Harrogate
Last Tuesday with a pair of his father's tups,
He came to me in my office and said:
"Judge, dost tha need any errands running
While I'm at spa?" "Son," I said, "if you'd be so kind
As to take this wig of mine to be repaired
You'd be rendering me an invaluable service."
What I didn't say was: "Keep it yourself
Then use it as a griming for your mischief
And leave it hanging in Mrs Rudd's trellis."

Bridget If you are cross-exampling me, your honour,
Let me answer you, I don't think Leslie's guilty.
He's my nephew, aye, but I'm speaking t'truth.

Martha But Bridget, chuck, I thought you said it were him.

Bridget Nay, what I said were I heard him near t'house.
I'm on my way to t'farm last night, tha sees,
To visit a niece of mine, who's with child.
And as I pass I hears Eve knocking about
And losing her rag with someone—in a huff,
She is, only trying to keep her voice down.
"What's up, Eve" I whispers through t'fence to her.
"Is summat wrong?" Tha could've heard a pin drop.
"Come on, love, answer me." "Hello, aunty."
"Is it Leslie wi' thee?" "Who else could it be?"
"Why doesn't he speak, then?" "It's all right, aunty,
You carry on, don't worry." "I'll carry on,
But you two had best stop your carrying on,
You're going at it like a pair of tomcats."
I say this all stern, to put t'wind up them,
But to myself I think, it's just a lovers' tiff,
They're close as inkle-weavers, ignore it.

Martha But this proves Leslie were with her.

Adam   Exactly.
Walter And then?
Bridget   I spend an hour nattering with my niece,
   And now I'm on my way back, near midnight,
   Under t'chestnut trees by Martha's garden,
   When knurr and spell, in a crack a demon bursts past,
   He's bareheaded, he's got a cloven hoof,
   There's steam coming off of him and he smells
   Of pitch and horsehair and fire and sulphur.
   The Lord preserve us, I cry, crossing myself,
   And turn round, my God, near scared to death,
   To see his bald head glowing through t'snicket
   Like a coal in t'fire you've taken a poker to,
   Then fading out of sight like an ember.
Leslie Good God alive! T'Devil himself were it?
Walter Mrs Howker, you're not seriously...
Bridget My eyes saw what they saw and my ears heard
   What they heard and my nose smelled what it smelled.
Tommy There've been other sightings, lately...
Martha   In Marton, aye,
   And Crosshills.
Leslie   They reckon bees-wax and hog's lard
   Is t'way to ward him off.
Martha   And pin-sticking
   And heart-frizzling.
Tommy   And wickenwood and bottery tree.
Leslie Hare's dung and owl's pellets burnt in a pan.
Martha Snail soup and bullock's blood.
Tommy   A toad tied on a belly
   Or spitting into t'mouth of a frog.
Walter Idle, superstitious Yorkshire guff.
   We live in a world of science and light now,
   Of machinery and logic and straight lines.
   Satan? No more about that old criminal,
   Please: everything must be subject to reason.
Bridget Nay, sir, there's a deep loam of witchcraft here
   And no machine will ever plough it up.
   I've known hedgehogs milk cows; I've seen hobmen
   Tramping t'lanes at dusk with their holly-sticks;

I've watched witches jump through their own keyholes
And scatter ill-fortune through whole towns.
There's nowt Yorkshire about it. In Lancashire,
You've your Pendle witches, and them's worst of all.
As to' t'Devil, ask Mr Bright, he'll back me.

Walter You'll back her?

Bright   Yes, sir, up to a point, sir.

Walter I give in. Not you as well.

Bright   With respect, sir,
If she could just conclude, uninterrupted.
The cloven hoof and the bald head and stench
—All this may turn out to be correct.

Walter Go on, then, Mrs Howker: I'll listen.

Bridget Well, I'm stood there in t'dark full of creepings
And shiverings and dodderums, when I hear t'brully
Coming from in t'house. You could have knocked me down
With a fillytail when Martha told me
What had passed. So I told her what I'd seen,
Then we go to t'spot where t'Devil appeared,
And in t'mud we can make out footprints. What kind?
I'll tell thee what kind. Right foot neat and dainty,
Just like a regular, common or garden foot;
Left foot a clumping, stumping, stumbling, hobbling
Great clod of a cloven hoof—Old Nick himself.

Tommy It were dark, though. Can tha be certain, Bridget?

Bridget I went back this morning at first light
And there they are in t'mud still, stepping out
In a crooked line, then through t'dew on grass,
Man's foot, Devil's foot, man's foot, Devil's foot,
Man's foot, Devil's foot, man's foot, Devil's foot.
When Mr Bright came to fetch me, I showed him t'prints.
Follow them, I says, and tha'll end up in hell.

Walter My God, all this lunatic peasant drivel.
And you were persuaded of this, Mr Bright?

Bright She was right about the tracks, m'lud.

Walter A cloven hoof?

Bright   No, two human feet,
But one somewhat resembling a cloven hoof.

Adam My word, sir, we're getting in hot water here.

I've read a few atheistic pamphlets
Arguing God doesn't exist, but as for Satan
I don't know who's ever disproved *him*.
This here's a secular court, with no brief
To muddle in matters ecclesisastical.
Us judge Satan? There's no point. He's been judged
Long since by t'good Lord Himself, and sent below,
And there's no sentence stiffer than that.
I reckon priests could help more than you or me.
I'd therefore propose that, rather than us risk
Some inflammatory theological verdict,
We refer this case to t'Synod in York.
Walter That's exactly the kind of proposal
I'd expect of you. What do you say, Mr Bright?
Bright Your honour won't need the Synod's intervention.
Just let the witness finish her statement.
Bridget   Mr Bright, I says,
These footprints are paving t'road to hell.
Maybe you're right, he says, let's test it out.
Nay, I says, that's one shop I'll not call at.
Worry not, he says, we'll not have to walk far.
Adam Mongoose...
Walter   And then?
Bridget   We started by t'chestnuts
Where t'Devil let out his fart of sulphurous gas
And damn near knocked me flat. There are marks in t'mud
Like t'kind a slinking dog makes round a cat
When she's arching her back and spitting at him.
Walter And then?
Bridget   Not far from there, ligging on t'ground,
He's left a little, er, memorial mound.
Being so scared, like, he must have had t'scutters.
Walter We don't need to go into precise detail.
It's where the tracks led I'm interested in.
Bridget Where they led? Straight here, like Mr Bright said.
Adam Judas.
Walter   To this court?
Bridget   Aye, from Martha's house,
Past t'castle, through t'graveyard, by t'cattle market,

Great clumps of earth to t'left, neat prints to t'right,
And bold as brass up to Judge Adam's back door.
Leslie Tha's not trying to make out t'Devil lives here?
Bridget I don't rightly know, but his tracks led here.
Tommy Maybe he passed through.
Walter   Were there tracks out front?
Bright Out front, your honour, there were no tracks at all.
Bridget Aye, tha could've eaten tha dinner off t'front step.
But on t'back, it were like he'd been muckspreading.
Adam Muckspreading? Aye, there's muck being spread here.
Who oversees t'cleaning of t'courthouse, eh?
Bright Me, sir, but...
Adam   "Me, sir, but..." Mr Bright and Clean, eh?
So why was there a great sleazy mess
On my back doorstep? It weren't there last night.
It must have been put there by someone—you.
Walter Judge Adam, you're diverting us from the path...
Adam Not at all, sir. We're talking blackmail here.
My clerk's after my job. What's power, I say,
But a lump of nowt inside a bubble?
That's not what he thinks; he plans to rise
By sinking me in t'mud. I'd venture to suggest
He could have smashed that pot himself.
Walter   Whooaah,
There's no evidence against him at all.
Adam Wait till you see his bookkeeping, m'lud:
It's more like novel-writing than accounts.
Walter To recap: the footprints were uneven,
Mrs Howker.
Bridget   Aye, like he were timber-toed, sir.
You know, a man with a gammy leg.
Walter Now good people, tell me, is there anyone
In Skipton whose feet are deformed?
Bright   Well, yes,
As it happens...
Walter   Who?
Bright   You'd best ask Judge Adam.
Adam I don't know what on earth he's on about.
I've lived in Skipton nigh on fifty year

And no-one's put a foot wrong anywhere.
Tommy What about Judge hisen?
Adam   Me?
Martha   Aye, you, Judge.
Adam Am I t'Devil, then? (*He shows his foot*) Is *that* cloven?
Can anyone say this foot's misshapen?
With a foot like this, that devil of yours
Could dance a jig at every hunt-ball going. (*He cavorts and dances*)
Bridget That's it! That's what I smelled, that's what I heard.
Martha Aye, but when was t'last time you saw t'Devil
Dolled up in white curls?
Adam   Alas, we in these parts
Know next to nothing of fashion trends in hell.
T'Devil has a fine head of black hair,
So they say—but I'd have thought when he comes
To visit earth, and hobnobs with t'bigwigs,
Then he dons a wig and coat-tails himself. (*He pauses*)
I trust this court is not under t'impression
That I, the judge, left my wig in that trellis.
Walter Heaven forbid. No, yours went up in flames,
As I recall, while you were studying.
Bright He told me another version, your honour,
That the cat he keeps had kittens in it.
Adam I see appearances conspire against me.
But as long as Eve refuses to speak,
I don't see how anyone can prove a thing.
Whoever says I'm guilty, come forward now
And swear it before this bench.

Pause

                              I rest my case.
Walter So will you now wind things up?
Leslie   Eve, was it him?
Walter Silence in court.
Tommy   Nay, he has a right.
Martha T'crafty old bastard.
Tommy Hauvey-gauvey. Bowdykite. Lapling.
Martha Bellyglut. Cauf-head. Lurdy.

Leslie Cloven hoof. Hebblewit. Rackapelt.

Walter Judge Adam, have you so little sense
  You can't see where these insults are leading?

Adam Right, I'm with you, your honour. If you'll allow
  I should now like to pass sentence.

Walter   Excellent.

Adam I've considered several possible pot-crackers:
  Higson, t'man with bow legs, maybe in York,
  Or maybe sidling back to clart round Eve.
  Leslie Dixon, t'accused, who said himself
  He were in Eve's room and has those gaping wounds.
  The tongue-tied Tommy Dixon, who wanted t'brass
  Back on t'ring. The witch-struck Bridget Howker,
  Tramping in t'lane with goblins when t'jug were broke.
  Dear, honest, Mrs Rudd, who thought her daughter
  Too good for Leslie and wanted t'banns called off.
  My clerk, Mr Bright, with his secret lust for Eve
  And machinations to unseat me from t'bench.
  Judge Walter, from t'wrong side of t'Pennines,
  Whose neck were cricked when he came to court first thing.
  Now weighing up all t'garfits and grime,
  I pronounce Leslie Dixon guilty of t'crime.

Walter Very good, go on.

Adam   His neck shall be placed
  In irons, and will remains so for three month.
  And since he were so ill judged as to insult t'judge
  He'll first receive fifty lashes.

Leslie   Three month?

Tommy Neck in irons?

Eve   Fifty lashes?

Bridget   For a jug?

Adam Aye, unless I boil him in oil an' all.

Walter Don't you worry, good people. Is that it?

Adam As for t'jug, whether he pays to replace it
  Is up to him—this court doesn't give a shite.

Walter Very good. This session is concluded.
  Any appeal may be lodged at the High Court
  In Manchester.

Eve   And in t'meantime…

Leslie   I'm in t'clink.

Eve (*to Walter*) Have you gone stark staring? Have you cracked?
You *know*, and you make out you're a judge, too.
Leslie, it *were* him—that clammy-clawed old malt-weevil.
Walter Silence in court.
Eve   Don't stand for it, Leslie.
It were Judge Adam cracked t'pot.
And that's while he were trying to crack me.
Leslie   Right, I'll have him.
Eve Aye, go on love, lounder him, skelp him.
Walter Stop this at once. Whoever disrupts this court
Will be severely dealt with...
Eve   So what! We've nowt to lose.
Your neck's on t'block, Leslie, so knock his off.
Adam If you'll excuse me, your lordship: it's been nice
Meeting you, but now I've some pressing business...
Leslie Stop him!
Eve   Sharp!
Bridget   Lucifer!
Martha   Lecher!
Tommy   Cat's collop!

Adam exits, evading his pursuers

Leslie Fuck it, he's got away, the horny goat.
All I've got's his empty bloody coat.
Walter Order in court. Let's have some order here.
Eve Your honour, if you don't help us we're lost.
Walter Lost? Why? I'm not going to impose the sentence.
Leslie is free.
Eve   That's still no good, he's lost.
Leslie Calm down, Evie. It's all right. What's up with thee?
Eve You've been called to t'army, that's what's up.
And not just off to France, fighting Boney,
But to Siberia. It's a secret.
Judge Adam told me.
Walter   Siberia? Never.
Eve Aye, to Siberia, sir, I'm not lying.
Look, here you are, here's t'letter in his robe,
From Downing Street, see, Judge has contacts there.
It says t'government has secret plans

To send new recruits out to Siberia.
It's all part of t'plan to beat Napoleon.
Judge Adam were helping: he were hanging on
To Leslie's papers so he wouldn't have to go.

Walter I've never come across anything like it.
Mr Bright, you tell them—have you received
The official call-up papers for Dixon?

Bright No, m'lud, any troops being called at present
Are doing their training in Catterick.
In any case, Leslie's name is not on the list.
And this stuff about Siberia here
Is in Judge Adam's own handwriting.

Eve The fiend, the fustilugs, the fuzzock,
The feggy, fudgy, flaumy, fliggery,
Flushy-faced, frummety, foxy old fffffff...
God, how he tricked me, I feel such a fondy,
I feel I've been lying in t'bottom of t'beck,
Dying to breathe and speak and tell someone,
Like I'd been stuffed down a pothole at Ingleb'rough
And somewhere, high up, there were light and air
And t'sound of lapwings, but I couldn't reach them,
There were this great weight pressing down on me,
No shifting it, like a shadow you can't lose.
I wanted to tell you, mam, you and all, Leslie,
But Judge Adam were always there, dogging me
And badgering me and giving me t'twitters
—If I'd nobbut do one tiny thing for him,
He could fiddle t'certificates, he said,
And save my Leslie from going into t'army.
On and on he went, wheedling and stroking me
Then asking could he come upstairs a while
To show it me in private, in t'bedroom,
Though what he tried to show me, and make me
Show him, that's summat no decent lass
Can ever speak of, it's that disgusting.

Leslie   To hell with him.
It's me that needs your forgiveness, love,
For all t'curses I heaped...

Eve   For doubting me.
That were t'bit that scaldered.

Leslie   For doubting you.
   If tha'll have me still, I'll not doubt thee again.
Tommy That's the spirit. Kittle and croodle and make up.
   I'll not get my brass back on that ring, but fine,
   Let's make it Whitsuntide for thy wedding.
Martha Aye. What's past is past. They've my blessing, too.
Bridget I told you they were close as inkle-weavers.
Walter He's hard to fathom is your Judge Adam.
   Mr Bright, I hope you'd feel confident
   About assuming his duties, if I asked.
Bright Me, m'lud? Well, I suppose I've had the training.
   I've studied his ways for nearly fifteen years...
   I'd be honoured, of course. Clear out of t'way,
   Dixon, lad: his lordship needs to sit down
   And discuss my future duties with me
   Now Judge Adam's been booted out.
Walter   Whooah there.
   Let's just say I'm temporarily suspending him.
   I don't want to force him from the profession
   Entirely, a man of his invention and skill.
   He has talents which could come in useful still.
Martha Your honour, could you tell me when and where
   I can go to t'High Court in Manchester.
Walter Why's that, Mrs Rudd?
Martha   For my jug, of course.
   How do you think it feels? I want it found
   My jug were t'innocent victim of a crime.
   Unless that's sorted out, its long years in t'world
   Have all been wasted and it's not even had
   A decent seeing-off. It came here for satisfaction.
   It's not had it, has it? It wants its rights met.
   Nay, tha's not heard t'last of this case yet.

Adam enters from the trap door, a dead bird in his hand

Adam You thought my cock were all bull, didn't you?
   Look at it: we're talking of t'murder of my pet.
   Nay, tha's not heard t'last of this case yet.

CURTAIN

FURNITURE AND PROPERTY LIST

Further dressing may be added at the director's discretion

ACT I

Scene 1

On stage: Bed
               Mirror
               Papers
               Pen
               Trapdoor
               Table
               Chairs

Off stage: Papers (**Martha**)

Scene 2

On stage: As before

Scene 3

On stage: As before

Off stage: Cracked pot (**Martha**)

Scene 4

On stage: As before

Off stage: Glass of ale (**Martha**)

ACT II

Scene 1

On stage: As before

Set: Lots of food and drink

Scene 2

On stage: As before

Off stage: Wig (**Bridget**)
Fake bird (**Adam**)

LIGHTING PLOT

Property fittings required: nil
1 interior setting throughout

ACT I, Scene 1

To open: Overall general lighting

No cues

ACT I, Scene 2

To open: Overall general lighting

No cues

ACT I, Scene 3

To open: Overall general lighting

No cues

ACT I, Scene 4

To open: Overall general lighting

No cues

ACT II, Scene 1

To open: Overall general lighting

No cues

ACT II, Scene 2

To open: Overall general lighting

No cues

EFFECTS PLOT

ACT I

No cues

ACT II

No cues